CREATED TO CONQUER

Roy

With best wishes

Elizabeth-Ann.

Also by Elizabeth-Ann Horsford

Complete as One

Created to Conquer

Personal Spiritual Warfare
Drawn from the Life of David

Elizabeth-Ann Horsford

Hodder & Stoughton
LONDON SYDNEY AUCKLAND

First published in Great Britain in 1996

10 9 8 7 6 5 4 3 2 1

British Library Cataloguing in Publication Data
A record for this book is available from the British Library

ISBN 0 340 66909 8

Typeset by Hewer Text Composition Services, Edinburgh
Printed and bound in Great Britain by
Cox & Wyman, Ltd, Reading, Berks.

Hodder and Stoughton Ltd
A Division of Hodder Headline PLC
338 Euston Road
London NW1 3BH

Contents

Acknowledgements   vii
Foreword   ix
Introduction   xi

1 The Battle Is On   1
2 Listen – Above the Sound of Battle   15
3 The Battle at Home   30
4 Keep Yourself Fighting Fit   45
5 Our Choices Are Important   59
6 Battling the Giants of Fear and Insecurity   68
7 Refusing the Works of Darkness   78
8 Pathway to Victory   97

Appendix I: Prayers for Use in Spiritual Warfare   107
Appendix II: Further Reading   111
Notes   112

Acknowledgments

I would like to thank the many friends who have prayed for me while I was writing this book and who have given me their valuable help and support. I have been conscious of your prayers on many occasions.

Most especially I would like to mention the blessing and encouragement I have received from my dear friends Clem and Miriam Mercer, who were always there to encourage me, pray for me and instruct me. From Clem's unique prophetic gifting I have learned so much and have been personally built up. He is now with the Lord; his battle is over, but the impact of his life will continue to affect the lives of many like myself. I am so glad, Miriam, that you are carrying on his much-needed ministry.

I would also like to thank Carolyn Armitage for her great encouragement and her painstaking work of editing and advising. My sincere thanks also go to Reona Joly, Helen Cooke, Ruth Giesner and John Schoneveld, who have read chapters and given much-appreciated advice and help. Many thanks also to Mary Cheetham for her contribution.

Lastly, and most importantly, I thank God for His enabling, His love and His protection, and for all He has revealed of Himself to me over the years. May this book be to His glory.

Foreword

In this fascinating and much needed study Elizabeth-Ann Horsford takes us on an enjoyable journey of discovery. She leads us into an exciting adventure of faith, inviting us to see our true purpose on earth. We have been called to live in close relationship with God and to be effective instruments in the dynamic fulfilment of his plans in the world.

This book offers us all a practical, no-nonsense approach to prayer, effective living and spiritual warfare. Avoiding dogmatic or slick step-by-step answers, Elizabeth-Ann leads us to find God's solutions for ourselves and, with the help of the Holy Spirit, apply them to our lives. Too often, books dealing with life's struggles are either merely a vehicle for the telling of super-star success stories or a depressing account of some personal tragedy. Neither approach offers the average reader anything of real value. The one is usually far removed from our ordinary experience as Christians and the other is often nothing more than one person working out their personal grief in public. However, in *Created to Conquer*, we have a fine piece of work that combines the caring and understanding nature of the author, who is not afraid to speak of her own trials, together with the firm and buoyant faith she holds in the triumphant nature of the Christian faith.

Above all Elizabeth-Ann places in our hands proven stones, like those in David's sling. These have been smoothed in the brook of her own experience and carried

on the bed of God's revelation to her. The story of David's
life is taken skilfully honed until every facet of our life and
experience before God is reflected there, leaving us with a
complete understanding of how God wants us to face these
crucial days in which we live. Whether we look on the inside
or to the world outside in the grip of evil, we know God is
shaping our lives as effective weapons against the enemy.
We are on the winning side!

Colin Dye
Kensington Temple

Introduction

The little girl knocked on the bedroom door and asked, 'Mummy, are you there?' But as there was no reply she ran quickly away, afraid to enter the room on her own.

I was the little girl, but why were my brother and I afraid to enter the bedroom on our own? It was in many ways a beautiful room, designed by our father, who had a passion for Chinese art. It had rice-paper walls, heavy red satin curtains with gold dragons on them, a bed designed by my father and made especially for him with a pagoda top and dragons at the feet, and even a built-in wardrobe painted with dragons and Chinese figures. Friends were invited in to see it, as if it were a museum piece. But there was something about that room that scared us children.

Right opposite the bed and looking down on it was a life-size wood-carved figure of a Mandarin with a beautifully painted robe and head-dress. My father had been given this figure as a present by someone who knew of his love of Chinese art, and it was his pride and joy.

One day my father was taken seriously and mysteriously ill, eventually losing consciousness. As he was a medical man himself (we lived in Harley Street at that time), he remained at home with a trained nurse to look after him, and his doctor came in twice a day. He continued to get worse and worse, and on one particular day the doctor told the nurse that he did not expect him to live through the rest of the day, and that when he came that night he would help her lay him out.

In the meantime my mother was getting phone calls from friends, quite naturally enquiring after my father. Having heard the news which worsened from day to day, they all ended with one question: 'Have you got rid of that Chinese figure?' – meaning the Mandarin at the foot of the bed. My mother would explain that it was something my father loved and that she was too worried to do anything about it now. But so many people asked this question that on the day when he was not expected to survive she phoned up the friends who had given it to my father and, explaining the situation, asked if they would have it back until he was better. They agreed, and the figure was removed from our house that very day.

On receiving it back, the daughter of the friends said to her mother, 'Isn't it strange that there seems to have been so much trouble ever since we had this figure? Soon after we got it father died. We lent it to a couple producing a Chinese play in London, and he and his wife were both killed in a car accident on the first night. And now Mr Horsford's ill.'

That evening, when the doctor came back to see my father, he said to the nurse, 'I don't understand this. I was certain he wouldn't make it through the day, but now he's getting better.' My father made a full recovery from his mysterious illness.

We never had the Chinese figure back, needless to say. Years later, when my mother was recounting this story to a missionary who had worked in an Asian country, he confirmed to her that such things were more than possible from his experience and from the experience of many. He suggested that the figure had probably been stolen from a temple and that a curse would have been pronounced on anyone handling this 'sacred' image.

My father had a number of friends who claimed to have spirit guides and were involved in the occult, and so from this early time I had a strong sense of the battle between good and evil.

Paul wrote that he was 'not unaware' of the devil's

'schemes' (2 Cor. 2:11). But it seems to me that in many ways we present-day Christians have allowed ourselves to be unaware and ignorant of his devices. Satan tries either to have us ignore him as though he did not exist or to fear him – we should do neither. We should follow Jesus's example in this: He was very aware of Satan's presence and wiles, but He did not fear him – rather, He overcame him. We see this in His overcoming of the temptation in the wilderness, His casting out of demons during His ministry and His defeat of Satan on the cross.

God made a perfect world and intended that it should remain so. It would have done if Adam, faced with the challenge of choice, had made the right decision and had obeyed God. He obeyed the wrong voice, unlike Jesus, the second Adam, who always chose to do His Father's will, and in so doing brought us salvation.

Satan's great desire has always been to bring mankind under his sway, to claim our worship and take the place of God. He tries to do this by lies and deceit and by casting doubt on God's Word and thereby on His integrity. The enemy asks us, 'Did God really say . . .?' He will do anything to discredit God in the eyes of mankind: 'Why did God let that disaster happen? . . . Why did God send that flood, that earthquake . . .?'

Why did Jesus weep at the grave of Lazarus, when He knew that He was going to raise him from the dead in a matter of minutes? I have often wondered about that. I favour the suggestion that I once heard Francis Schaeffer give: Jesus wept in anger at the intrusion of death which came into the world as a result of the entrance of sin.

This is not in any way to say that God is not all-powerful and in control of His universe. His ways are far above our ways and His thoughts are far higher than our thoughts; nothing takes Him by surprise, and His purposes for us and the world will be fulfilled.

In the meantime, if we understood more about the strategies of Satan we would be more likely to be on our guard against him and to be less ignorant of his devices, and therefore more able to appropriate the victory of

Christ. For example, who is behind the quarrelling and back-biting in a church? Or the coldness and apathy of many Christians towards the lost? Who is instigating the violence in our society and the growing interest in witchcraft and the occult?

We might ask, 'Why are we still in a battle when Christ gained that great victory on the cross, which was to destroy the works of the devil?' Mankind was put on this earth to have 'complete authority' over it (Gen. 1:26 Amplified Bible). When man sinned, he gave over that authority to the one whom he had obeyed – Satan. Jesus Himself referred to Satan as the 'prince of this world' (John 14:30).

Now we are in a battle to win back that authority and to resist the evil one. At the cross Jesus struck the crucial blow – Satan was defeated. But he has been allowed to stay and have limited power for what purpose? God allows the warfare so that through it He might bring us into the likeness of Christ, who always chose to do His Father's will and who loved righteousness and hated wickedness. Jesus told us to pray for the coming of God's kingdom and will on earth (see Matt. 6:10), and as we allow God to work in our hearts to establish His kingdom there, we shall see the answer to that prayer on earth.

In Judges 3:1–2 we read that all those who had never known war were trained for war, and David himself several times attributes his training in warfare to God (see 2 Sam. 22:35; Pss. 18:34, 144:1). Paul also reminds us that we are in a spiritual battle, not fighting against flesh and blood but against principalities and powers and spiritual forces of evil (Eph. 6:12). And they are very real. I only wish I had known some of these things years ago in my ministry.

The purpose of this book is to highlight personal spiritual warfare, as through various means Satan tries to rob us of the joy and peace and fruitfulness which God wants us to have and which are ours by our new birthright. He also tries to thwart God's great plan to make us like His Son, Jesus, who was 'more than a conqueror' (Rom. 8:37).

King David, on whom this book is based, is probably one of the most colourful characters in the Scriptures and in history. He had the unique privilege of being called a man after God's own heart (Acts 13:22). There are many lessons that we can learn from him in our own spiritual warfare. As he was a man with similar passions and problems to ours, may we come to realise that we too are created to conquer.

Chapter 1

The Battle Is On

As Eliab, David's eldest brother, woke to another day of cloudless sky his first thoughts were, 'Today will be different. It *must* be different. Surely the breakthrough will come today. O God, let it be today!'

And then he heard it. That earth-shattering, terrifying sound. The voice boomed out as it had done every day for six weeks. Not again! Not another day of this relentless taunting which struck such fear into the hearts of these soldiers: 'Choose a man and have him come down to me. If he is able to fight and kill me, we will become your subjects; but if I overcome him and kill him, you will become our subjects and serve us . . . This day I defy the ranks of Israel! Give me a man and let us fight each other' (1 Sam. 17:8–10). This continual taunting caused terror and dismay in Saul and his army. No wonder it did – their opponent was nine feet tall and was well skilled in warfare.

Let today be different! How many times have we all felt that, when faced with some seemingly insurmountable difficulty or some long, on-going, intractable problem? But this day *was* to be different.

Away on the distant Judean hills was a young shepherd boy. He was insignificant in the eyes of his family and despised by his brothers, but in God's eyes he was a king in the making. How wonderful that God can take the least significant of us and make us His man or woman and use us to fulfil His purposes for mankind. That was true of this

shepherd lad named David. The youngest son of Jesse of
Bethlehem, he had been given the job of tending the sheep
while his brothers went off to war in Saul's army. He was
not even considered important enough to have been invited
to the momentous family feast which Samuel called for when
he was sent by God to Bethlehem to choose a king, as we
shall see later. He was misunderstood and reviled by his
eldest brother, Eliab.

Yet God was preparing him for a unique role in history.
He would take this young shepherd lad and make him into
Israel's greatest king, through whose line God's own Son
would enter the world. Jesus said, 'I am the Root and the
Offspring of David, and the bright Morning Star' (Rev.
22:16). Because of his important role in history Satan
would do his utmost to try and destroy this man through
outside influences and inward weaknesses. But up there on
the hillside David was learning to know his God in a deeply
personal way. He experienced His power and protection
when fighting off the lion and the bear that attacked his
sheep, and he learned an intimacy with his God that would
one day enrich the world through his psalms. He learned
to be an overcomer as God prepared him for all that would
lie ahead.

Satan attacks us today for the same reason – to try to
destroy the purposes of God, but we too can overcome his
attacks. Now, on this particular day, David's father, Jesse,
had another job for him. He was to leave the sheep and go
and see how his brothers were getting on at the battle front,
and he was to take a gift to their commander. As David
arrived he was impressed to see the army of Israel going
out to its battle positions, and he was very proud to see his
brothers among them. But what is this? The mighty men of
Israel, resplendent in their armour, ignominiously scurrying
for cover as their nine-foot adversary taunts them yet again!
'What are we going to do?' they ask. 'How can we overcome
this man?' 'There isn't a man among us who would be able
to fight him. None of our men are near his stature. Most of
us are hardly trained in comparison to this man, who has
been a man of war from his youth. We're sunk!'

As all the negative thoughts came to the surface and caused dismay and panic, the young, inexperienced lad who knew nothing about war accurately summed up the situation. He looked at it not at ground level, where giants always look big, but from the place he had been in so often – the heavenlies. How did God view this situation? Young David recognised the issue at once: 'What will be done for the man who kills this Philistine and removes this *disgrace* from Israel? Who is this uncircumcised Philistine that he should defy the armies of the living God?' (1 Sam. 17:26). He was the only one who realised the most important thing of all – that this was a direct attack on the honour of God and that it should not be tolerated at any price. The Israelites were the people of God, but instead of setting the battle rules themselves, they allowed the enemy to call the strokes, and so they were set for defeat.

Stand your ground

David was fearless about meeting Goliath because of his confidence in God. Out on the sheep hills he had learned some very important lessons. Because he trusted in God and had a close relationship with Him on those lonely hills, he was unafraid when danger came. He knew that under God he was stronger than the enemy. So we read in 1 Samuel 17:34–35 that when the lion and the bear came and took a sheep from the flock, David 'went after it, struck it and rescued the sheep from its mouth'.

When the backlash came, as it often does, he knew how to deal with that too: 'When it turned on me, I seized it by its hair, struck it and killed it' (verse 35). He caught the animal in a vulnerable place – by its hair, near the face – and killed it. Very often we allow Satan to set the agenda for us. He attacks and reminds us of something in the past, for instance, and we agree with him, allowing ourselves to get down and to lose that round. The other day someone reminded me of something I had done in the past which I had regretted. It came like an arrow – a fiery dart – and I smarted. As I left that person I was reminded that the matter had already been dealt with at the cross, that I was already forgiven and free, 'So let it go!' I didn't let it go but continued to smart under it for some time. And I felt aggrieved at the person. Then I realised what was happening and why. A few days before that took place I had been asked to become a personal intercessor for a Christian leader who was at that time abroad on a very intensive tour. I had been having great freedom in praying for him and had been able to follow him closely in prayer. But now something had come in to upset and distract. Unlike David, I was slow in taking the enemy by the hair and killing it. But when I did, I was able to continue in intercession.

How many times we let ourselves be pushed into a corner by Satan and allow him to get away with it through fear and often through shame, as his accusations always have some truth in them concerning our shortcomings. But if we think biblically we can put him to rout. In my case, with a situation already dealt with at the cross, I needed to remind myself that 'there is now no condemnation for those who are in Christ Jesus' (Rom. 8:1).

We need to ask the Lord to help us quickly to discern the attacks of the enemy; to be more alert at strategic times, such as during special intercession or in preparing for some service for the Lord; and to realise that the attack comes not from the person but from the demonic influences at work at that time. How many rows might have been averted if instead of being angry with the person and being determined to get our own back we had recognised the power behind the remark or situation and had attacked that instead of the person. Paul reminds us in Ephesians 6:12 that 'our struggle is *not* against flesh and blood', but so often we forget that and attack the person.

David, undeterred by the scorn and criticism of his elder brother, refused to be deflected from his searching question about Goliath. Finally he was brought before King Saul, who also treated him with a certain amount of scorn and incredulity that such a strip of a lad could really think of taking on this giant. But in the end he decided to let him try, and so he clothed him in his own armour:

Then Saul dressed David in his own tunic. He put a coat of armour on him and a bronze helmet on his head. David fastened on his sword over the tunic and tried walking around, because he was not used to them.

'I cannot go in these', he said to Saul, 'because I am not used to them.' So he took them off. Then he took his staff in his hand, chose five smooth stones from the stream, put them in the pouch of his shepherd's bag and, with his sling in his hand, approached the Philistine.

(1 Sam. 17:38–40)

Over the last two or three years I have read many, many books on spiritual warfare written by internationally renowned authors, and they have been of great help and instruction. I have also attended seminars on the subject which have been invaluable. But in the final analysis, from whom does one learn about spiritual warfare and intercession? There is only one source – God Himself – and He will teach and lead you according to *your* anointing, not someone else's. We can learn a great deal from reading – hence the bibliography at the back of this book, recommending a number of books that I consider to be important reading on this subject. But we cannot and dare not think that we can go into spiritual warfare with someone else's anointing. We need to know our weaponry, and our own giftings and limitations.

A good example of someone who relied on her own anointing and not on another's is the life of Suzette Hattingh. She was converted at the age of twenty-two in her native South Africa. She now has a ministry of teaching intercession to thousands, and she is responsible for the intercessory back-up for all of the campaigns of the evangelist Reinhard Bonnke. How did she learn about intercession? To begin with she was a busy nurse and had little time for anything else, but in her days off, not knowing where to go for fellowship, she just went to her room, locked the door, got on her knees and prayed and read the Bible.

She read very few books apart from the Bible and spent time learning from God. The result? God made her into a highly effective intercessor and trainer of intercessors. Many, like myself, have benefited from her ministry, as she has travelled to many parts of the world teaching people to pray effectively.

David's weaponry

David took some stones and a sling – weapons he knew how to handle – and depended totally on the God he had proved he could trust. Hadn't God helped him on the hillside when his sheep were attacked by the bear and the lion? If God had helped him then, surely He would help him now.

Five flat stones would be laughable to any soldier, even in those days. 'David, you're crazy. It may have worked in the hills with the animals, but now you're dealing with a sophisticated, highly trained, exceedingly powerful man!' Saul said something like that to him before he went out to meet Goliath. Saul said, 'You are not able to go out against this Philistine and fight him; you are only a boy, and he has been a fighting man from his youth' (1 Sam. 17:33).

How many of us have been put off by discouragements like that from within ourselves or from others? 'What can I do?' 'Who do you think you are?' Satan is always asking us who we think we are and making derogatory remarks about us. Unfortunately, most of us agree with him. Not so David. He concentrated on the greatness of His God – an undeniable fact, even for Satan.

See his bold assertion to Goliath after Goliath had despised him and cursed him:

> I come against you in *the name of the LORD Almighty*, the God of the armies of Israel, whom you have defied. This day the LORD will hand you over to me, and I'll strike you down and cut off your head. Today I will give the carcasses of the Philistine army to the birds of the air and the beasts of the earth, *and the whole world will know that there is a God in Israel*. All those gathered

here will know that it is not by sword or spear that the LORD saves; for the battle is the LORD's, and he will give all of you into our hands. (1 Sam. 17:46–47)

David had already prepared for this battle on the hills of Judea, so when the time came he was confident.

We read that he picked up five stones. There are those who feel that this was due to lack of faith, that he should only have picked up one. I beg to differ. It seems to me he was being a wise steward of his resources – he went out prepared. Could it also have been a prophetic act, as Goliath had four brothers who were all eventually killed by David and his men? (See 2 Sam. 21:19–22.)

As I prayed over what these stones could possibly represent to us in a practical way, five things came to mind that are essentials if we are to be overcomers in our Christian lives:

1. Obedience and submission to God at all times.

2. Knowledge and application of the Word of God. That means not just knowing what the Bible says but living by it.

3. Constant communion with God – through prayer and waiting upon Him. In spiritual warfare it is essential that we move only on God's orders, as we shall see in Chapter 2.

4. The fullness of the Holy Spirit. We are talking about spiritual warfare, and we can only meet spiritual forces with spiritual weapons (see 2 Cor. 10:4). We cannot do this without the Holy Spirit, and the greater His fullness in us, the greater the power at our disposal.

5. Holy boldness – that is, using the authority vested in us. This is not the same thing as presumption!

David only used one stone, but I believe all five were important, as all those five qualities listed above are vital in our lives. We may never know which one is the one that gives the final blow to the enemy, any more than David knew which stone he chose – that is not important. What is important is that all these characteristics need to be in our lives and growing if we are to be victorious in our warfare and in our daily living.

Know your identity in Christ

On David's victorious return with the head of Goliath, the
first question Saul asked him was, 'Whose son are you?' (1
Sam. 17:58). It was important to Saul to know the credentials
of the one who was coming into his service.

It is also an important question to the enemy. In Acts 19
we read of the seven sons of Sceva who, having seen the
miracles being done by the apostles, thought they could
copy them and tried to drive out a demon 'in the name of
Jesus, whom Paul preaches' (verse 13). The demon replied,
'Jesus I know, and I know about Paul, but who are you?'
and the men were overpowered. They were using the name
of Jesus but without His authority, because they did not
know Him. It is vitally important in spiritual warfare that we
know who we are in Christ and that we know the authority
which He has given us.

When we became Christians we moved from Satan's
jurisdiction to God's, and we are now under new ownership.
Satan hates this and will do all in his power to undermine
and neutralise our effectiveness for the kingdom of God.
He will often do this by making us feel so unworthy and
ashamed that we feel we could never be used by God, and
certainly never be loved by Him. This is Satan's biggest
lie, and it is important for us to recognise it. We need to
know the truth of what God has said in His Word – 'This
is love: not that we loved God, but that he loved us and
sent his Son as an atoning sacrifice for our sins' (1 John
4:10). And we need to believe it, because it is true, and we
need to keep it in our heart and mind so that we can use it
as an effective weapon against the lies of Satan, much as
David used his stone.

When Satan reminds us of our past sins we can remind
him that we are now a new creation in Christ – the old things
have passed away and the new has come (2 Cor. 5:17). We
need to remind *ourselves* that we have been 'blessed . . .
with every spiritual blessing in Christ', that we have been
chosen by him (Eph. 1:3–4), that because we are in Christ
we can approach God 'with freedom and confidence' (Eph.

3:12), that God has given us 'a spirit of power, of love and of self-discipline' (2 Tim. 1:7).

I have found it helpful to write some of these biblical statements down in a small notebook which I carry with me. I read them over at times when I am feeling pressured or down, and reminding myself of the truth of them gives me renewed hope and courage.

The armour of God

Paul tells us in Ephesians 6:11 that we need to have on us 'the full armour of God', not Saul's armour or some earthly protection which is useless. There is nothing about us that would ever impress Satan. Our church-going, or our good works, or our theological degrees will never stand up on their own against Satan's craftiness.

Paul, who had more than his share of learning and orthodoxy, was the one who warned us to be clad in God's armour. First of all he mentions the belt of truth. This, if you like, was the foundation garment. The Roman soldier, with his flowing tunic, would catch it up in a belt when going into battle to save him being tripped up in his own garments. We need to make sure that truth – the truth of God's Living Word, Jesus, and of His written Word – is the foundation of our lives, if we are to be victorious against the enemy of truth.

Right from the beginning of time Satan has tried to get us to doubt the Word of God. To Eve he said, 'Did God really say, "You must not eat from any tree in the garden"?' (Gen. 3:1) – a doubt sown and a misquote given. He tried exactly the same thing with Jesus in the wilderness, but Jesus, who is the Truth (see John 14:6), overcame him with the Word of truth (see John 17:17). Jesus claimed that if we know the truth, the truth will set us free (see John 8:32) – free from the lies and domination of Satan.

Many people are being deceived today by false cults, the New Age movement, the occult in its various forms, the subtle and not-so-subtle influences of the media, and the fact that today certain behaviour is accepted that would not have been accepted years ago, such as sex outside of marriage, homosexuality, divorce, illegitimacy – to mention a few. Society tries to make us believe that because 'everybody's doing it' it must be all right. But everybody was 'doing it' in Sodom and Gomorrah, but that did not change the judgment of God any more than our behaviour today will make Him change His mind to accommodate modern standards. 'I the LORD do not change' (Mal. 3:6). Let us thank God that in this world of change and faithlessness He is unchanging and faithful, and yet in His love His arms are outstretched to receive us as we turn from our sin and go to Him. Let us have our hearts and minds filled with the Word of truth, as surely as having a firm belt around our waist, like the Roman soldier, to avoid being tripped up.

Speak the truth

Another aspect of the belt of truth is the importance of our own truthfulness. In spiritual warfare it is imperative that we seek to lead holy lives, as known and unconfessed sin in us leaves us unprotected. We will look into this further as it is clearly shown in David's life, particularly in his sin with Bathsheba. Following the uncovering of this sin by Nathan the prophet, David acknowledged to God, 'Surely you desire truth in the inner parts' (Ps. 51:6). We must be open and honest in our dealings with others, avoiding the 'little white lies' which are not white in God's sight, nor are they little!

For example, the phone rings. A child goes to answer the phone, and on the way he or she hears a trusted voice say, 'Tell them I'm out!' 'Mummy lied . . . and in the process, so did I!' What does that do to the child? And as he or she grows older, bigger lies will come more easily and naturally, because that is the accepted way of life.

Our excuse might be, 'But I was genuinely busy cooking' or whatever it was that we were doing at the time. Then what about saying, 'Tell them Mother's not available right now'? That was the truth and would usually be acceptable to the person who was phoning.

Or the Christian businessman, wanting to make a good deal and finding himself being economical with the truth in order to sell his products, may well find in the course of time, to his cost, that 'Those who honour me I will honour, *but those who despise me will be disdained*' (1 Sam. 2:30), as the faulty product is exposed or the shady deal is uncovered, with all the attendant shame and hurt, often involving many innocent people.

Watch your heart

The next piece of armour was the breastplate of righteousness. The breastplate covered the chest and the heart, the most vital of our organs. No soldier would think of going to battle without it. It was like the bullet-proof vest of today. As this is the Armour of God, it is not our righteousness that forms the breastplate, but Christ's. Our righteousness has been likened to rags, and filthy ones at that (see Isa. 64:6), and they would be no defence at all against the weaponry of the enemy. But, wonderfully, we are clothed in Christ's righteousness, and against that Satan has no armoury. It has been rightly said that there is nothing in us that would impress the devil. But he is awed and overcome by the righteousness of Christ. Paul reminded us that the righteousness of Christ comes to us by faith and not by the law. So when Satan, the great legalist, reminds us of our own shortcomings and seeks to condemn us, like Martin Luther, we may have cause to agree with him, but also like Luther, we can remind him that we are now clothed not in our own righteousness but in the righteousness of the One who has already sealed the devil's fate. That should call forth praise from us, which is one of the most powerful weapons in spiritual warfare.

Be sure-footed

Next we have the shoes of 'the readiness that comes from the gospel of peace' (Eph. 6:15). How important it is to wear protective and stable footwear that will help us to further the

gospel. 1 Peter 3:15 tells us that we should always be ready
to answer the question concerning the hope that is in us. 'Let
the redeemed of the LORD say so, whom he hath redeemed
from the hand of the enemy' (Ps. 107:2 AV). It is because
you are a sinner saved by grace, warts and all, that you can
speak. People watch to see how you react to unfortunate
things, or how quickly you apologise when you have done
something wrong or when there is tension between you and
another. Maybe the other person was wrong, but you, as a
Christian, should take the initiative, bringing an apology
and seeking to put things right.

When the going is hard and we are perhaps suffering from
illness or some other problem, it is important to have our
feet well shod with the firm foundation of the Scriptures, so
that we will not be 'tossed about by every wind of doctrine'
or every storm of adversity. When we get sick, how often
we ask, 'Why me?' 'It's not fair. What have I done to deserve
this?' I have found it more helpful to say, 'Lord, what do
you want to teach me through this?' God has promised to
give us the treasures of darkness (Isa. 45:3), and very often in
the darkest places of suffering or difficulty God reveals His
greatest treasures and insights about Himself that cannot be
learned in any other way. David had many bitter moments
in his life, but through the Psalms we see how he turned to
the Lord and received not only encouragement but also the
ability to give to future generations some inspired writings
that have helped and encouraged millions through the ages.
We need to turn to God's Word for our stability.

The shield of faith

The shield of faith will help us in our stormy times too.
The Roman shields were large, covering the whole of the
body. They were usually made of leather and then soaked
in water, so that when the fiery darts of the enemy came
they were immediately extinguished when they hit the shield.
Another thing about those shields is that they all locked
together, so that when the enemy advanced the soldiers
would stand shoulder to shoulder with the shields locked

into one another, and thus they would be able to withstand the onslaught. And the row of soldiers behind gave cover for the back.

How do we extinguish the fiery darts of fear, uncertainties, doubts and insecurities? By holding up the shield of faith. It depends not on how much faith I have, but on who my faith is in. When my faith is firmly grounded in the eternally faithful One and in His unchanging and dependable Word – 'Forever, O LORD, Thy Word is settled in heaven' (Ps. 119:89 AV) – then, whenever the enemy's fiery darts of doubt or fear come, I can withstand them with the Word of faith.

Protect your mind

Next comes the helmet of salvation to protect our head. Our minds are constantly under threat from what we see and hear, and we need to be discerning as to what we allow in and what we reject in our choices of what we watch, read or listen to. In 1 Thessalonians 5:8 Paul talks about this helmet as 'the hope of salvation'. We need to constantly remind ourselves during the battle of the hope laid up for us in heaven (not a vain hope, as many of our earthly hopes are, but a certain hope), which can never be taken from us. Satan is the god of despair; our God is the God of Hope.

Keep your sword sharp

Lastly, we come to the sword of the Spirit, which is the Word of God. This is not only a defensive weapon; it is also the only offensive weapon in the armour. We need to use the sword of the Spirit, God's Word, in overcoming our own temptations and demonic attacks, following the example of the Lord Jesus in the wilderness, when each time He foiled Satan with the reply, 'It is written . . .' It is the Word of God that will help us overcome the enemy, not our own arguments. When you are on the spiritual offensive – for example, praying for your city or town or for a person in spiritual bondage – praying the Word of God is very powerful.

To keep the sword from going rusty I would strongly recommend the memorisation of Scripture. This is one of the most useful and powerful things I have done in my Christian life, and many others can testify to the same.

Make sure the armour is constantly on you. I like to go through it every day, putting it on in my mind's eye as I speak it out to myself. It is true that you should never take it off – who would consciously do that? – but I find it very helpful, particularly in certain situations I might be facing, to remind myself of each of these pieces of armour and to make sure they are in place. I also pray for discernment, a most important weapon in spiritual warfare, so that I may be quick, like David, to recognise the target of Satan's attack – namely, the honour of God.

Chapter 2

Listen – Above the Sound of Battle

One of the great characteristics of David's life and a frequently recurring phrase in his story is that 'he enquired of the LORD.' He involved God in every area of his life and asked His guidance and wisdom before making major decisions. There are two or three notable instances, which we shall also consider, when he didn't ask God, and we see the tragic results that followed, not only for him but also for others. I believe this matter of enquiring of the Lord is a very important factor in spiritual warfare. 'What is God saying in this situation?' 'What is the cause of this difficult problem?' These are questions we may need to ask and get an answer to before we can begin strategic praying.

Asking God's direction

In 2 Samuel 2 we see that David even asked God where he should live, and having received specific instructions, he went and settled in Hebron. At an earlier time in his life, when David was told that the Philistines were attacking the walled town of Keilah, he immediately asked God if he should attack the Philistines. David was by then experienced in fighting and very successful in it too. After all, wasn't that the cause of Saul's jealousy? 'Saul has slain his thousands, and David his tens of thousands' (1 Sam. 18:7). And yet he wisely refused to lean on his past experience, but got fresh direction from the Lord. God said, 'Go, attack the

Philistines and save Keilah' (1 Sam. 23:2). 'Great!' thought David. 'It should be plain sailing from now on.'

But no. When he shared this piece of guidance with his men they were horrified. 'David, you're crazy!' they said. 'You've got this all wrong. We're already scared enough here in Judah. What in the world are we going to be like if we go out against the Philistines? Think again, man!'

So what did David do? Did he abandon the whole project? 'Yes, they're right. I must have misheard. It must have been wishful thinking. It's just my personality. I always like to help the underdog so it was probably just my own thoughts.' No, he didn't abandon it. He did another wise thing. When doubts and uncertainties came to him because of what people had said, he went back to the Lord and asked Him again. 'Did I really hear you right? My men are scared to death. What do you want me to do?' And again the Lord answered him, this time with an added assurance: 'Go down to Keilah, for *I am going to give the Philistines into your hand*' (1 Sam. 23:4). The result? They went down, and all that God had said would happen did happen, of course.

Later on David was pursued by Saul, and here we see an interesting contrast between the two men. David and his men were now in a walled city, and so they were in a dangerous position from a military point of view, since they could easily be attacked there. Saul assumed that this was God's doing (1 Sam. 23:7).

How often we are tempted to assume that something is God's will because 'it looks right' or our reason tells us that this must be so, when all the time God's plans are very different, and if we took time to ask Him we would know.

All through Saul's life it seems this was one of his weak points. He didn't take time to enquire of God, but followed his own desires and feelings, and when at the end of his life he did enquire, God appeared not to listen, so he turned to a medium. What a tragic contrast to David.

At Keilah David was in a dangerous position, but when he heard that Saul was plotting to besiege the city and capture him and his men, he again enquired of the Lord, this time asking God some very honest questions, all of which received unpalatable answers. 'Will Saul come down . . . Will the citizens of Keilah surrender me and my men to Saul?' (1 Sam. 23:11–12). To both questions God answered 'Yes'. It was not what David would have wanted to hear, but having heard, he took action and was saved from the hand of Saul.

It seems that today we do very little enquiring of God. So often we wonder why our prayers were not answered, why people we prayed for were not healed, why the job sought and prayed for did not materialise, and so on. And often it has resulted in shaken faith: 'What's the use of praying?' we say. 'Where was God when I needed Him?' And yet we do need to ask ourselves the question, 'Did I take time before praying to ask God what He wanted in this situation?'

Over thirty years ago, a young mother, feeling a burden to pray, joined with a friend, and together they listened to God and prayed accordingly, and as a result the Lydia Fellowship came into being.

At the time of writing it has spread to over seventy countries throughout the world. One of the great blessings in my life over the last five years has been to belong to Lydia and to be part of a prayer group which meets weekly (some groups meet more or less often than this) to intercede for the nation and the world. From them I have learned so much about the importance of waiting on God and seeking His mind if we are really going to be effective in prayer. At each meeting, after a time in the Scriptures, we ask God to show us what He would have us pray for concerning the nation, instead of coming with our agendas. After a time of quiet prayer we often find that a couple of us have been impressed with the same topic, and there follows a time of concentrated intercession, and often there is further revelation on the subject.

How should we pray?

We need to know in our own lives what God is saying to us, and we need to seek His will for others if we are praying for them. How many of us have prayed for friends to be healed, only to see them die? We feel shattered not only by their death but also by the seemingly 'unanswered prayer'. A few years ago, two dear friends of mine were stricken with rather virulent forms of cancer. We all prayed. In one case, I asked the Lord, 'How should I pray for her? Are you going to heal her?' I felt the Lord say deep in my spirit, 'No, I am going to take her.' Not long after that I had dinner with this friend and she talked to me very triumphantly about death, and how she was looking forward to it (she was a lovely Christian, so why not?). Her pastor's wife phoned me soon after this to ask me for any insights I might have about how they should be praying for her, as several people in the church had really been urging prayer for healing. But she had no peace about it, and so she asked me what I thought. When I told her my conviction, she said she felt that this confirmed in her spirit what God had said to her. Not long after that our friend died peacefully.

In the case of the other friend, I asked God to show me how to pray for her while I was on my way to visit her in hospital. My answer did not come until I was with this friend, and it came through her. As we were talking together she said, 'God has not promised to heal me, but He has said I am going on a beautiful journey, and He will be with me.' As I left the hospital I thanked the Lord that He had given me His answer. My friend has now completed her beautiful journey.

These may seem rather depressing stories, but I wonder if we should think of them like that. For the Christian, death is entering into the glorious Presence of our wonderful Lord whom we have started to come to know here. Knowing Jesus here and now is so wonderful, and yet it is only a minute foretaste of what is to be. We are so earthbound! I sometimes wonder if the Lord is not saying, 'All these Christians say they love me, but so few of them want to be with me where I am!' The moment illness strikes, the first thing we do is to rush for healing. Just a thought!

On the other hand, there are countless numbers of people

who have been healed, some known and some unknown to us. We can confidently know that God is in the business of healing, and we can see it happen in this day and age in answer to prayer. But we need to know the mind of God in each situation.

A year after surgery and radiotherapy for breast cancer, I developed very severe back and hip pains and was scheduled to return to the hospital for a bone scan. A friend whom I asked to pray about this situation said, 'You haven't been looking very well lately.' Thanks for the encouragement!

I was scared. Was God telling me something through this, and even through this comment? I decided I had to enquire of the Lord. So I went to the place in my home where I usually pray and asked the Lord specifically, 'Lord, has my cancer come back [thinking, "If it has, He saw me through it the last time, so He'll see me through it again"] or has it not? Lord, I need to know.' I did not say, 'Lord, please tell me everything is all right.' That would not have been asking God anything, but telling Him, 'I don't want an honest answer – I want a nice one.' I had to be willing even for an unpalatable answer.

The comfort of God's Word

As I waited before the Lord I sensed that He was saying to me, 'It is not cancer but don't talk about it.' Following that thought, the story of the Shunamite woman came into my mind, and I even had to look it up in my concordance to see where it was in the Bible (2 Kings 4:8–37). I read it every day for ten days at the beginning of my morning quiet time, and I was greatly blessed. When her child died this woman did not even tell her husband (who would, no doubt, have ordered an immediate funeral). She asked permission to go to the man of God, from whom she knew she would receive help. And God raised up her son and restored him to her. She did not allow anyone to fuel her fears, but kept on until she reached Elisha and the help she needed. Let us always test the word God speaks to us in our heart by the Bible. He never says anything which is contrary to His written Word.

We often hear the phrase, 'A problem shared is a problem halved.' While this is often true, it is also true that sometimes a problem shared is a problem doubled, as well-meaning people come to us with ideas we hadn't even thought of to 'encourage us', whereas in reality they scare us to death! I believe that was why God told me not to talk about it, as people's reactions could have increased my fear.

Later, when I went for my bone scan, the doctor said he had seen the X-rays but could tell me nothing, because 'Your doctor will want to discuss it with you.' A momentary panic hit me. But again I felt the Lord speaking to me and saying, 'Are you believing him or are you believing Me?' I said in my heart, 'I'm believing you, Lord,' and peace was restored. I had to wait for three weeks before I received the happy result – that there was no further cancer.

You may ask, 'What has all this got to do with spiritual warfare?' Everything. As we see from the life of David, one of the most important ingredients of spiritual warfare is knowing what God is saying and not rushing ahead or holding back. We must not be presumptuous and go and do battle for the Lord where He has not called us, nor should we hold back if God is calling us to take issue on a certain matter. The old saying, 'Evil triumphs when good men do nothing' is so evident in our society today. Therefore we need to know what God would have us pray for individuals and for our nation if we really want to see things happen. Jesus told us to pray, 'your will be done on earth as it is in heaven' (Matt. 6:10). Very often God gives us insight about a certain person or situation for whom we are praying, and at the time it might seem a strange thing to pray, but then God shows us as He answers that our prayer was right on target. I remember one time when I was uncertain about my future and what I should be doing, suddenly finding myself praying, 'Lord, please show me, by letter tomorrow.' Having prayed it, my first reaction was,

'Oh! Whatever made me pray that? Now I'm really tying God down.' But I somehow felt it was a prayer which the Holy Spirit had prayed in me. And sure enough, a letter landed on my door-mat the next day inviting me to a new job in Christian work, which I accepted.

So often after a time of blessing, the devil attacks us in a most vicious way. In 2 Samuel 5 we read that immediately after David had been anointed king of Israel at Hebron, the Philistines came to attack him: 'they went up in full force to search for him, but David heard about it and went down to the stronghold' (verse 17). He then asked God whether he should go and attack the Philistines and whether God would give them into his hand. As the answer to both these questions was 'Yes', he went into battle and was victorious.

Be open to change

In the next verses we learn a very important lesson. After the battle was over the Philistines gathered again in the valley. How easily David could have thought, 'Well, it worked last time, so there's no need to pray about this again. Let's go and lick them once more.' But David was both a wise and godly man, and so once more he turned to prayer to ask God what he should do. It was a good thing that he did, because this time the instructions were quite different. Of course, the enemy would have been more prepared for him this time and would have been anticipating his attack, so a change of tactic was necessary. How many good works for God have died on their feet because of the fear of change, and the cry, 'We've always done it this way!' has resounded as they have disappeared into oblivion.

This time God told them not to go straight at the enemy but to circle around them and to move only when they heard 'the sound of marching in the tops of the balsam trees' (verse 24). God would go before them to strike down the enemy. He did, and a mighty victory ensued. F.B. Meyer remarks, 'The movement in the trees suggests the footfalls of angel squadrons. Oh, for the quick ear to detect the goings-forth of God's help, and grace to bestir ourselves to follow!'[1]

What if they had not waited? I wonder how many of us are willing to have our direction changed over something that has worked well with us for many years, but now God is saying either 'Lay it down – I want to do something new' or 'The same thing but a different method.'

David's tragic mistake

One time when David did not consult the Lord disaster struck. In the very next chapter following the success of these two battles we read that David now wanted to bring the Ark up to Jerusalem – the sacred vessel which God had given to Moses in the wilderness and which was the symbol of the Presence of God with His people. In 2 Samuel 6:1 we read that David brought together 30,000 chosen men. If there's safety in numbers, he certainly had it! In 1 Chronicles 13 we read that David conferred with his army commanders concerning the bringing up of the Ark. He formed a committee of men who, though powerful and effective in military matters, had no idea of the spiritual implications of bringing up the Ark, and although the decision to proceed was unanimous (therefore surely it must be right!), it resulted in disaster. In 2 Samuel 6 we read an account of what happened. David had the Ark placed on a new cart, and the procession began with much praising and celebrating. As they went along, the oxen pulling the cart stumbled, and it looked as though the Ark would fall off. So understandably, Uzzah put his hand out to stop it, touched the Ark and immediately dropped dead.

We read that David was angry. Was he angry with himself for not having asked God for guidance to do it properly? If he had done this and consulted the priests instead of the military, he would have known that God had specifically commanded that the Ark should be carried by the Levites and not put on a cart: 'The Kohathites are to carry those things that are in the Tent of Meeting' (Num. 4:15). When we wilfully disobey God's Word there is always trouble.

Attack after blessing

Later, when David saw how God had richly blessed the man who had housed the Ark, he decided to try again. This time he got it right. The Levites were to carry the Ark, as commanded, and he admitted that his failure had been in not asking God's guidance in the first place (see 1 Chron. 15:13).

As they joyfully entered Jerusalem with the blessing of God upon them because of obedience, the happy occasion was somewhat marred for David by the bitter taunt of his wife as she saw him dancing before the Lord, openly praising God and celebrating. And why hadn't she been present to join in the celebrations with the other women?

Often in the midst of blessing, and even while we are praising God, we can experience the enemy's attack. How we handle it is all important. We can let it get us down, and then all praise stops – 'Why did God let that happen?' – and we find ourselves blaming the wrong person. Or, like David, we can stand our ground and refuse to be pushed into a corner. David dealt with his wife's criticism, and apparently God did too: 'And Michal daughter of Saul had no children to the day of her death' (2 Sam. 6:23). Was this a one-off attitude problem or was it something more deeply ingrained? We will explore this further in a later chapter.

The importance of doing God's will, not ours

Two other times when David did not seek the Lord for guidance also brought him to disaster. The first was his sin with Bathsheba, which we will look into in more detail in Chapter 4. But at the moment let us look at it from the standpoint of the importance of seeking God's guidance for our daily lives.

In 2 Samuel 11:1 we read: 'In the spring, at the time when kings go off to war, David sent Joab out with the king's men and the whole Israelite army . . . But David remained in Jerusalem.' And from then on, as we see in the story, David fell morally and committed a double sin – adultery with Bathsheba and the murder of Uriah – and we read, 'the thing David had done displeased the LORD' (verse 27).

We see no evidence here that David asked God, 'Shall I go to war this spring? Or shall I send Joab instead?' He perhaps rationalised, as we often do: 'Joab needs the experience. I've done enough. Surely I deserve a break. There are things I need to look to here.' All good excuses, but none of them are valid if they are contrary to God's wishes. How different this whole story might have been if at this point David had asked God for His guidance. And how the devil made full use of the situation! He knows our weak points and will always seek to exploit them, so we need to be constantly on our guard against such attacks, and we must make sure that we do not put ourselves directly in temptation's way, as David did.

Then there was David's attempt to count the people, which turned out to be a national disaster. We read of this in 2 Samuel 24:1, where it states that because God was angry with Israel, He incited David to number the people. The same incident is recorded in 1 Chronicles 21:1, where we read, 'Satan rose up against Israel and incited David to take a census of Israel.' From these seemingly conflicting accounts we see that God is in ultimate control of everything, allowing Satan limited power for now. So nothing happens to you or me without God's permission. Remember, Satan had to get permission from God before afflicting Job, and from Jesus before sifting Peter: 'Simon, Simon, Satan has asked to sift you as wheat. But I have prayed for you, Simon, that your faith may not fail. And when you have turned back, strengthen your brothers' (Luke 22:31–32).

Why was God angry with Israel? Before David numbered the people, he had not come before the Lord and said, 'This is what I want to do. Do I have your permission?' I believe that if he had done so, God would not have given permission, but instead would have revealed to David why He was angry with Israel and what should be done to make amends. It is interesting to note that in the 1 Chronicles account we read that Joab, himself not an exemplary character, nevertheless

warned David concerning the evil he was about to commit.
But to no avail. David's ears were closed to God and to all
good advice. And so Satan was given permission to take the
matter into his hands. Sometimes, when we are under fierce
attack from the enemy, we do need to ask, 'Have I done
something to allow this?' And as we seek the Lord with
a sincere and repentant heart, He will show us if there is
some cause. Obviously, that is not always the case, and
often before or after times of blessing the devil particularly
attacks us. So we need to be on our guard especially at
such times.

David came to his senses and acknowledged his sin: 'Then
David said to God, "I have sinned greatly by doing this.
Now, I beg you, take away the guilt of your servant. I have
done a very foolish thing"' (1 Chron. 21:8). As there was
no immediate military threat at this time, was it pride that
motivated David to number his army (a long and costly
business that took over nine months), or was it that at this
time he was relying more on the military might which he
could muster in an emergency than on God? It could have
been both, but whatever the case, David realised that his
motive was at fault.

Through the prophet Gad, God gave him three choices
of punishment – three years of famine, or three months of
running before his enemies, or three days of plague. David's
response was characteristic: 'I am in deep distress. Let me fall
into the hands of the LORD, for his mercy is very great; but do
not let me fall into the hands of men' (1 Chron. 21:13).

So the result of David's sin was three days of intense
plague in which 70,000 people died. What anguish he
must have suffered as he saw his people dying as a result
of his sin.

Surrender of ambition

As David's victories increased and his kingdom became
established, he had a great desire in his heart to build a
permanent resting place for the Ark – to build a house for
the Lord. That desire came from a heart devoted to His

God and from a passion for His honour. So he called in his trusted spiritual adviser, Nathan, to see what he would say to the idea. Nathan responded as many of us would have been tempted to respond. He thought, 'Who's asking me? David's been close to the Lord for years. He's a praying man. He won't get it wrong.' So Nathan replied, 'Whatever you have in mind, go ahead and do it, for the LORD is with you' (2 Sam. 7:3). But like many of us, the next morning Nathan had to eat his words. He had not stopped to ask God before answering, so God had to tell him later; he then had the difficult task of taking back a very different and disappointing reply to David, that it would not be him but his son who would be the one to build a house for the Lord (2 Sam. 7:13).

I am always impressed by David's amazing and joyful acceptance of this thwarting of his ambition, when he could well have been jealous of his son and bitter against God. No wonder God called him a man after his own heart. Not only did he pray a wonderful prayer of praise and worship to God (which we find in 2 Sam. 7:18–29), but he also made every possible preparation for his son, Solomon. What a noble and big-hearted man. How many of us sometimes side with Satan in this battle and get angry with God when He does not do what we ask or 'tell' Him to do, forgetting that His ways are perfect and that He knows the end from the beginning and what is best for us too.

No second cause

Some years ago, while I was working with a Christian organisation abroad, during a big reshuffle I was passed over for a leadership position which I had been led to believe would one day be mine. It was a very shattering experience. I talked it over with a trusted friend who was also a member of the church I attended at that time and who had had a similar experience. After listening sympathetically, she then said, 'You do know, don't you, that the whole church is looking to see how you take this.' It was like someone throwing a bucket of cold water in my face! But, just like a bucket of cold water, it really woke me up. It took my mind off myself, and I was able to see that what we were dealing with here was God's honour. If I fell apart and got angry and bitter, it wouldn't do anybody any good and it would dishonour God. So I thanked her and took her words to heart. God healed and God blessed, and the years that have followed have shown very clearly that it would not have been right for me to be in that leadership position. Hudson Taylor said, 'There is no second cause but God', and I believe that too. When we realise that, we can keep Satan from robbing us of our joy and peace, and we can have a sense of security in knowing that God does have our best interests at heart and knows what He is doing.

Let us learn to be like David, and take time to find out what is on God's agenda for us and for those for whom we pray. However, we do need to ask the important question, 'How can I know that it is God who is speaking to me?' There are many things and people out to deceive us today, and we do need to be careful.

Surrendered to God

The first thing we need to be sure of is that our lives are surrendered to God – that we know Him not just as Saviour but also as Lord. In Romans 12:1–2 we read some crucially important words:

> Therefore, I urge you, brothers, in view of God's mercy, to offer your bodies as living sacrifices, holy and pleasing to God – this is your spiritual act of worship. Do not conform any longer to the pattern of this world, but be transformed by the renewing of your mind. *Then you will be able to test and approve what God's will is – his good, pleasing and perfect will.*

Make God's Word your guide

Then we need to test everything with the Word of God. Does what I believe I am hearing from God fit in with what He teaches in His Word? Is God ever likely to give directions contrary to 'Thou shalt not commit adultery' or 'Thou shalt not covet thy neighbour's wife'? I think not.

But many Christians today behave as though He suddenly changed the commandments just for them. No wonder we are in the sad situation that we see around us in the Church today. You may not always get a direct word from Scripture in answer to a question such as, 'Shall I go to America?' America doesn't appear in the Bible, but God can guide you through His Word in principle. I have found this to be true many times – for example, following my prayer about cancer, as I explained earlier. I lived on the story of the Shunamite woman for days, and it fed me and protected me and kept me close to the Lord through difficult circumstances.

In all aspects of spiritual warfare and of spiritual growth the Word of God is essential, or else we will fall. 'I have hidden your word in my heart that I might not sin against You' (Ps. 119:11).

Testing the word from the Lord with godly and trusted friends is very helpful, but do remember Nathan's advice to David *before* God spoke to him!

Jesus gave us that lovely promise in John 10:27: 'My sheep *hear* my voice, and I know them, and they follow me' (AV). We need to spend time hearing his voice, and we need to have a heart and mind which are ready to listen to him. We need to clear away the clutter in our lives – for example, too much TV watching, constant radio listening when doing the chores at home, indulging in mental arguments instead of praying for the person you would love to argue with. What do you think about when you are vacuuming the house, washing the dishes, making the beds, going to pick up the children from school? What occupies your mind as you drive to or from work, or as you go to see a business client? A difficult business deal could be turned round as a result of fifteen minutes of prayer in the car on the way, instead of talking on the mobile phone! These are just examples, but whatever our life or work entails, and however busy we may be, there are far more opportunities than we realise for listening to God – and how often we miss them! These are all valuable moments when we can be in prayer, focusing our mind on God and listening to Him. I have often enjoyed times of prayer and hearing from God when driving along the motorway. It's good to listen to teaching and worship tapes, but sometimes we need to switch off the tape player and ask God to speak to our hearts directly.

In the next chapter we will consider one of the major battlegrounds in spiritual warfare – namely, the family. It was created by God to be a place of harmony, peace and security, and therefore it is a major target of Satan.

Chapter 3

The Battle at Home

'God gave us our relations. Thank God we can choose our friends.' That amusing saying expresses the heartfelt feelings of many, which are expanded upon in books such as *Families and how to Survive Them* by Robin Skynner and John Cleese.

From the beginning of time the family was designed by God to be a place of harmony, security and nurture. In many cases, thank God, this is a wonderful reality. But we also see that the family is under attack. Not only are marriage breakdowns increasing, but so too is child abuse, both physical and sexual. The first murder took place in the first family when Cain, through jealousy, murdered Abel, his brother. And today police statistics tell us that a large percentage of homicides are domestic.

Satan knows that if he can strike at the family and destroy that structure, then he is a long way towards destroying a nation. When discipline breaks down in family life or is non-existent, lawlessness in the nation is not far behind. We can see in our society today many examples of the things expressed by Paul to Timothy concerning the last days: 'People will be lovers of themselves, lovers of money, boastful, proud, abusive, *disobedient to their parents*, ungrateful, unholy, without love, unforgiving, slanderous, without self-control, brutal, not lovers of the good, treacherous, rash, conceited, lovers of pleasure rather than lovers of God' (2 Tim. 3:2–4).

As we are moulded by our upbringing and family life, it is not surprising that Satan would do all in his power to try to spoil the work and purposes of God in our lives from the beginning. And yet let us keep in mind the wonderful fact that 'The reason the Son of God appeared was to destroy the devil's work' (1 John 3:8). This is another reminder that we are in a battle. The war is on, and we need to be aware of what is happening and we need to take action.

David's early years

Let us look into David's family. David was the youngest of eight sons, and as he grew up he was given the task of minding his father's sheep. The nation of Israel was going through a difficult time, as Saul had been rejected by God as king. Moreover Samuel, the prophet of God, on whom they had all relied, was not often seen around these days because of the turmoil in the nation and because he was grieving for Saul (1 Sam. 15:35).

In the midst of this turmoil, God spoke to Samuel and told him to go and anoint one of the sons of Jesse of Bethlehem as the new king. So suddenly, and much to everyone's consternation, Samuel appeared on the scene again in Bethlehem. Even the elders of the town 'trembled' when they met him. 'Do you come in peace?' they anxiously asked (1 Sam. 16:4). He reassured them by telling them he had come to sacrifice to the Lord, and all those who would be present were to make special preparations before coming. It was a solemn and important occasion. David's father, Jesse, was no doubt especially honoured when Samuel himself consecrated him and his sons and invited them personally to be present at this great occasion. It would also appear that Jesse knew that Samuel was going to choose one of his sons to be king (see 1 Sam. 16:8), so why was David not included in this very important family event, but was off tending the sheep as usual? 'He's too young, he doesn't really count. He's always been difficult. He was an after-thought. We didn't really want him. He was an accident, an unplanned pregnancy.' How often have we heard that said either about us or others. I remember speaking at a meeting, and a woman came up to me afterwards with her adorable two year old and said to me in his presence, 'This is my unplanned pregnancy'! I wondered how many times that child had heard those words. He did not yet understand what they meant, but he soon would, and I wondered what effect it would have on his life later.

I am constantly appalled as people tell me that they were not wanted, not expected, a nuisance to their parents. How did they know? Their parents told them. To what purpose? Even if the child is loved now and has been brought up in a loving family relationship, it is still very damaging to be told that, and Satan delights to use it all through a person's life, unless they are cut free from that by prayer. If you are in that situation, don't let it continue to rancour. Ask a trusted Christian friend who has knowledge of these things to pray with you and for you, to cut you free from the negative effects of such comments.

I wonder how David felt up there on the hillside that day tending the sheep, when he would have known what was going on in the town below. When David later wrote, 'Though my father and mother forsake me, the LORD will receive me' (Ps. 27:10), was it referring to their death or perhaps to an episode like the one just described? Certainly, Jesse did not think of him in any way as a possible future king, and so seemed surprised when none of his other sons fitted the bill.

Some scholars have suggested that David may have been illegitimate, as suggested by his statement, 'Behold, I was shapen in iniquity; and in sin did my mother conceive me' (Ps. 51:5 AV). If that was true, then that could be another reason why he was not included in this all-important feast, thus relieving his father of further embarrassment and possibly a family row. Certainly, we understand from the Bible narrative that his father was old when David was born, and his brothers didn't have much time for him – especially Eliab, the eldest.

You can just imagine the scene. First, Eliab comes before Samuel. He probably remembered how Saul was chosen for his physique, and so as he stood tall and proud he was probably thinking, 'Surely I will be chosen. I am the eldest, I have a fine physique. Surely I am the one!' What a shattering blow it must have been when he was by-passed. And all the other brothers would have felt the same. And then Samuel asked, 'Are these all the sons you have?' – a moment of embarassment and shuffling of feet! On hearing that the youngest was out tending the sheep, Samuel said, 'Send for him; we will not sit down until he arrives.' What an honour for David. But we can imagine the thoughts of Eliab! 'Oh, no! Not him! He's such a conceited little brat. He doesn't count. He may be nice-looking, but he doesn't have the presence and physique that I have. And what preparation does he have for being king? He just spends all his time with the sheep, making up songs with his stupid harp.'

They forgot that 'Man looks at the outward appearance, but the LORD looks at the heart' (1 Sam. 16:7). They were also totally unaware of the painstaking preparation by God of the future king and his strategic role. As the psalmist Asaph wrote: 'He chose David his servant and took him from the sheep pens; from tending the sheep he brought him to be the shepherd of his people Jacob, of Israel his inheritance. And David shepherded them with integrity of heart; with skilful hands he led them' (Ps. 78:70–72).

I have often felt how deeply wounding it must have been for someone with as tender a heart as David to be left out of such an important family gathering. 'God has chosen me and I'm honoured and grateful. But my family, from whom I long for love and understanding, think nothing of me.' Was it the craving for love from his earthly father which created in him his passion for God? How often the things which we find difficult in our lives can produce the best fruit, if we let them.

Later, when David went at the request of his father to see how his brothers were faring in the battle (as we saw in Chapter 1), Eliab very soundly put him down. He overheard David asking what would be done for the one who killed the Philistine and removed the disgrace from Israel. 'When

Eliab, David's oldest brother, heard him speaking with the men, he burned with anger at him and asked, "Why have you come down here? And with whom did you leave those few sheep in the desert? I know how conceited you are and how wicked your heart is; you came down only to watch the battle'" (1 Sam. 17:28). Could it have been jealousy that promoted that outburst? David's reply implies that this was not an isolated occurrence: 'Now what have I done? Can't I even speak?' (verse 29). He did not allow himself to be intimidated by this, nor did he become angry and sulky, but he turned aside to pursue his enquiries, which eventually brought him to King Saul. How Satan delights to sidetrack us by having us react to nasty remarks and comments. We need to be aware that what he is doing is to divert us from pursuing the matter in hand, because he knows its importance. David knew a major battle was ahead, so he was determined not to engage in a small and unimportant one which would have distracted him and occupied his mind on lesser things, and thus deflected him from the very purpose for which God had brought him to the battle on that day.

Dealing with hurts

Many people have been emotionally scarred and deeply wounded by parents or siblings, and this can make their lives especially vulnerable to satanic attack. For example, a child who experiences violence in the home can develop a deep spirit of fear and hatred of authority which carries over into adulthood and can cause much anguish. Or a child who is unloved by his or her parents can grow up with a feeling of rejection and an inability to love or receive love from God or people. How many people grow up with deep insecurities through lack of encouragement or the constant put-down from the one from whom they most needed and desired approbation?

Some parents, especially mothers, can show love in a manipulative way, indulging ultimately in emotional blackmail. God commanded that we honour our father and mother, and so we should, but Jesus also said, 'Anyone who loves his father or mother more than me is not worthy of me' (Matt. 10:37). Satan, because he always seeks to thwart the purposes of God and undermine the people of God, has often used parents to produce guilt in their offspring, by letting them know they can never do enough, and by reminding them of all that has been done for them, and thereby bringing a burden of debt upon them that God never intended. Barbara Johnson, in one of her books, said, 'My mother was a tour guide for guilt trips,' and I wonder how many of us can identify with that. I suspect many more than would admit it. Because we are emotionally bound up with our parents, it is very often hard to see the fine line between fulfilling our duty to them willingly, lovingly and rightly, and being under the emotional domination of a demanding parent which will take us beyond our rightful duty and into bondage and self-condemnation.

I believe this is a major area that Satan uses, and I have seen many people, especially women, who have been dominated by their mothers, and they have never felt free from it, even after the mother's death. It is nearly always the aspect of guilt that comes in and causes wrong judgment and wrong actions and certainly wrong attitudes. 'I feel guilty because I get angry with my mother's demands, and yet I cannot do more than I am doing . . .' If you identify with any of this you may need to talk this through with somebody you trust and who would pray with you and give objective advice. There needs to be a cutting off of the emotional bonding if it is that strong, so that you can, in a godly way and not in an emotional way, serve your parents. As we put the Lord first and then our parents, and not the other way round, God will enable us to honour them in the right way. How many marriages have been wrecked because the commandment to leave and cleave has been disobeyed? 'For this reason a man will leave his father and mother and be united to his wife' (Gen. 2:24; quoted in Matt. 19:5 and Eph. 5:31).

It is also sadly true that many marriages have been wrecked by parents who have refused to allow their children to 'leave and cleave', but still feel they have the right to interfere and control two adults who, first and foremost, should be committed to each other. On that important occasion when Samuel came to anoint one of his sons as king, could it be that Jesse deliberately left David minding the sheep, hoping that David, being the youngest, would stay with him and care for him in his old age?

David's dysfunctional family

Years later, after many triumphs on the battlefield and many wonderful experiences of God, many of them recorded in the Psalms, and his great example of being a man who 'enquired of the Lord', it is sad to see the disarray in David's family life and the disgraceful behaviour of his sons. One of them, Amnon, raped his half-sister Tamar, and then was murdered by his half-brother Absalom. We read that when David heard of the rape of Tamar 'he was furious' (2 Sam. 13:21), but apparently he did nothing.

It is perhaps surprising to realise what a poor father he was, when one considers that here was a man who gathered around him 'all those who were in distress or in debt or discontented' (1 Sam. 22:2) and turned them into an effective fighting force (1 Sam. 23:5) and yet he could not control his own sons. Could it be that his experience of family life, as we have seen, had affected him as a father?

In their book *Forgiving Our Parents and Forgiving Ourselves*, Dr David Stoop and Dr James Masteller state:

> We recognize that our parents had their flaws and our family its weaknesses, but we have never felt that our adult lives have been negatively affected by them in a major way. Most people who place themselves in this category are surprised when they discover how big the 'little' hurts they endured are, and the effects they have had on their lives.[2]

Many parents either re-enact what they have seen their parents do (often wishing they didn't, but feeling unable to control the situation), or react out of the hurt they have received. For example, a parent who never received love as a child will either be distant from their children, unable to show love, or will lavish too much love or manipulative love to over-compensate for what they did not receive. Both extremes can be devastating to the child and can be a real battleground for spiritual warfare later on. The childhood hurt needs to be recognised and acknowledged – 'I am hurting over this' – and the parent or person responsible for the hurt needs to be forgiven, or healing will not take place.

Many people find it hard to acknowledge that their parents might have been wrong, but just have a niggling feeling that something is wrong or a mild, lingering depression, or anger. If this is true of you, ask God to show you the problem, and be prepared to face it and not sweep it under the carpet. I remember talking with a young woman once who had had a great sorrow in her life, largely due to the behaviour of a parent. Instead of acknowledging it, she would merely say, 'I'm better off than many people.' Although this may have been true and sounds very heroic, it did nothing to relieve her of her sorrow and problems. It never does.

We must come and honestly confess our feelings to God, in the same way as we can only receive forgiveness for our sins from God by acknowledging them and not making excuses – 'I'm not as bad as others.' That also may be true, but it is not an excuse that will stand up before God. David himself understood this when he said in Psalm 32:3, 'When I kept silent, my bones wasted away through my groaning all day long.' But in verse 5 he experiences the wonderful fact of forgiveness: 'Then I acknowledged my sin to you *and did not cover up my iniquity*. I said, "I will confess my transgressions to the LORD" – and you forgave the *guilt* of my sin.'

Failure to deal with sin

Two long years passed and Tamar lived in her brother Absalom's house as 'a desolate woman' (2 Sam. 13:20). Still

David did nothing. Then Absalom thought up a deceitful plan to invite all his family, including David his father, to a big banquet following the sheep-shearing. Absalom had had two years to think up his plan and to allow the hatred of his brother to grow. And the hatred of his father. No doubt he considered his father largely responsible for what had happened to Tamar, by sending her to tend her brother. Normally a princess would not do a menial task like preparing food, so it was an unusual situation which ended in tragedy. His father's lack of action to punish Amnon led Absalom to despise him and sowed the seeds of his later rebellion and bid for the throne.

Why did David not discipline Amnon? Was it because of his own sin with Bathsheba? Did he think, 'I dare not say anything because of what I did, therefore my hands are tied'? How often Satan will shut our mouths by reminding us of past sins that have already been forgiven. Nathan had warned him that there would be trouble in his household: 'I will take your wives and give them to one who is close to you, and he will lie with your wives in broad daylight' (2 Sam. 12:11) – referring to what Absalom would later do: 'So they pitched a tent for Absalom on the roof, and he lay with his father's concubines in the sight of all Israel' (2 Sam. 16:22) – yet Nathan also said after David's confession, 'The LORD has taken away your sin' (2 Sam. 12:13). We must not let Satan push us into a corner and remind us of things which God has dealt with, and in our case, cleansed by the Blood of Christ. David should have taken a firm stand with Amnon and meted out justice and dealt with the sin right away, and so prevented the further evils that followed.

Later, David's son Solomon was to write, 'Because sentence against an evil work is not executed speedily, therefore the heart of the sons of men is fully set in them to do evil' (Eccl. 8:11 AV). Perhaps he had these events in mind. Following the death of Amnon the same pattern follows. Absalom fled to Geshur, part of the vassal state of Syria within David's empire. He could easily have sent for him to bring him to justice, but again he failed to do so. On this occasion he mourned deeply for his son, until his general Joab, disturbed by the behaviour of the king, which could also have endangered the nation through lack of alertness to enemy attack, contrived a cunning plan to bring Absalom back. By a bit of play-acting on the part of a 'wise' woman, David was at last persuaded to allow his son to return to Jerusalem (not that he had ever banished him – Absalom went of his own accord). But even this did not accomplish much, because although Absalom was back in Jerusalem, longing to see his father, yet his father refused to see him. 'Absalom lived for two years in Jerusalem without seeing the king's face' (2 Sam. 14:28). To show how desperate Absalom was to see his father, after having twice sent for Joab to come and Joab refusing, he got his servants to set fire to Joab's field, producing the desired effect. Joab came to him and arranged an audience with the king. We are told very little about this interview, merely that 'the king summoned Absalom, and he came in and bowed down with his face to the ground before the king. And the king kissed Absalom' (2 Sam. 14:33).

Reconcilation and repentance are necessary

Was there real reconciliation, repentance and asking for forgiveness on both sides? David for failing in his fatherly and kingly duty in seeing that justice was done after Tamar's rape, and Absalom for having taken the law into his own hands in killing his brother. It is interesting to note Absalom's comment to Joab in verse 32: 'if I am guilty of anything, let him put me to death.' How graphically that illustrates the terrible condition of having a conscience which has been 'seared as with a hot iron' (1 Tim. 4:2). Such a conscience is dead, unable to feel or distinguish between right and wrong. Such a person is open to all kinds of deception and is also a ready tool for Satan to use.

How often do we hear of people who, after committing adultery and going off with someone else's spouse, say, 'We don't think we have done anything wrong' – and this from Christians! This grieves the heart of God and gives more ground to the enemy.

In 2 Samuel 15 a clue about what happened at the interview is given, as we see Absalom conspiring to steal the hearts of Israel away from his father and to himself. Things went from bad to worse, and eventually David left his home and his city and took to the hills again. What made David, who as a young man had fearlessly faced the giant Goliath, run from his own son? We will explore this in more detail in a later chapter.

As David left the city, it seems that he was dogged by further deception. Mephibosheth, Jonathan's crippled son, to whom David had been so gracious, in the end let him down (2 Sam. 16:4 and 19:24–30). David was also cursed by Shimei (see 2 Sam. 16:5–14), an incident which is also dealt with in a later chapter.

Later, after Absalom had been killed and the battle had been won, we see David's excessive and possibly remorseful grief which nearly brought about the downfall of his kingdom. The day of victory for Israel was turned into one of shame: 'Joab was told, "The king is weeping and mourning for Absalom." And for the whole army the victory that day was turned into mourning . . . The men stole into the city that day as men steal in who are ashamed when they flee from battle' (2 Sam. 19:1–3).

The ravages of remorse

There does seem to be a striking contrast between this time of unbridled grief for his dead son Absalom and the time when David prayed and fasted for his son by Bathsheba during the child's fatal illness. In both cases one might say that David was responsible for the deaths, but in the case of Bathsheba's son, through his prayer and fasting and subsequent acceptance it seems he had allowed God to do a work in his heart, bringing deep repentance and worship. 'Is the child dead?' he asked. 'Yes,' the servants replied, 'he is dead' (2 Sam. 12:19). Then David got up from the ground. After he had washed and put on lotions and changed his clothes, he went into the house of the Lord and worshipped. Then in answer to his servants' bemused question, he explained, 'While the child was still alive, I fasted and wept. I thought, "Who knows? The LORD may be gracious to me and let the child live." But now that he is dead, why should I fast? Can I bring him back again? I will go to him, but he will not return to me' (2 Sam. 12:22–23). One is reminded here of Paul's words: 'Godly sorrow brings repentance that leads to salvation and *leaves no regret*, but worldly sorrow brings death' (2 Cor. 7:10).

Now, as he grieves over Absalom, we see the worldly sorrow at work. Of course, it would be right and understandable to grieve for his dead son, but it seems that possibly much remorse entered and sullied the grief. Guilt after a death is a cruel tyrant and brings the grief to levels which are impossible to bear without the knowledge that with God there is forgiveness and mercy. Satan can use remorse as a major inroad into our lives, as he tried to with David, and because of these unguarded moments in David's case it would have cost him his kingdom, had it not been for the timely intervention of Joab. His words may seem harsh: 'Today you have humiliated all your men, who have just saved your life . . . You love those who hate you and hate those who love you . . . I see that you would be pleased if Absalom were alive today and all of us were dead' (2 Sam. 19:5–6). But sometimes strong words are needed in desperate situations: 'Now go out and encourage your men. I swear by the LORD that if you don't go out, not a man will be left with you by nightfall. This will be worse for you than all the calamities that have come upon you from your youth till now' (verse 7).

What parallel can we find in our own life and in relation to spiritual warfare? Absalom seems to me like a form of self-indulgence, or dreams of the future not given to us by God, but produced by our own imaginings and longing. When they are not fulfilled we grieve and indulge in self-pity, blaming God and condemning ourselves and bemoaning what might have been. This is unhealthy and dangerous, as it gives occasion to the enemy to come in and agree with us and give us that sense of frustration and anger because *we* did not get what *we* wanted, and feeling that all the fault is ours, but God could have helped us too. We need to realise that frustration is annoyance at our inability to be in control of our lives and circumstances.

Who's in charge?

But who is in charge of our lives and circumstances? When I am feeling frustrated and irritated about things in my own life, I find great comfort in the words of Jesus: 'Take my yoke upon you and learn from me, for I am gentle and humble in heart, and *you will find rest for your souls*' (Matt. 11:29). This shows us that we need to be walking close to the Lord in obedience and putting others before ourselves, and then we can experience the freedom of knowing God's control and guidance and the fulfilment of doing His will, not ours, and therefore fulfilling our eternal destiny and not our ethereal dreams. When we cling on to our desires and allow frustration to eat into our souls, then we too will be unable to stand before the enemy.

It was only when King David was received back by his people that the kingdom was once again established and secure. Have we brought the King back to his throne in our own hearts? Only then can we know protection and security against the enemy.

The final picture we see in the life of David concerning his family comes with yet another son, Adonijah, trying to usurp the throne like Absalom had done. Here again we get another insight into David's seeming lack of fathering skills when we read in 1 Kings 1:6 about Adonijah: 'His father had never interfered with him by asking, "Why do you behave as you do?"' And the uncorrected and undisciplined young man sought to gain the power and authority which he considered to be his due. He was, after all, now the eldest son, but God, who knows the hearts of all men, had already chosen Solomon and had made that choice known to David. Adonijah was crowned king and the situation was only saved by the intervention of Nathan the prophet and Bathsheba, who reminded the king, now old and infirm, of the promise he had made concerning his son Solomon. God's word to David, like all His promises, would stand: 'you will have a son who will be a man of peace and rest, and I will give him rest from all his enemies on every side. His name will be Solomon, and I will grant Israel peace and quiet during his reign' (1 Chron. 22:9). Even right up to the end Satan will seek to snatch the empire of the world for himself, but God has given his solemn promise to His Son: 'Sit at my right hand until I make your enemies a footstool for your feet' (Ps. 110:1).

So we can see that . . .

1. We are moulded by our families. They are the closest to us, and from them we need approbation. We are dependent on them from the earliest years, and some find it hard to be separated from that dependency throughout the rest of their lives. That is why the death of a parent or parents can be devastating to some people.

2. Our family background and upbringing does affect how we are, and in many cases the experience of our upbringing has been good and positive. But there are many people for whom this would not be true. If you are one of them, then to you I would say, don't let this dog your footsteps for the rest of your life. Acknowledge the problem honestly before God. He knows what sort of parents you had and He knows how to turn the ugliest situation into one of blessing for you and for others. Remember that the very purpose for which Jesus came was to

> bind up the broken-hearted,
> to proclaim freedom for the captives
> and release from darkness for the prisoners . . .
> to comfort all who mourn,
> and provide for those who grieve in Zion –
> to bestow on them a crown of beauty
> *instead of ashes*,
> the oil of gladness
> instead of mourning,
> and a garment of praise
> instead of a spirit of despair.

(Isa. 61:1–3)

Take God at His Word and believe it, because it's true. And don't let Satan rob you any further of the joy, peace and fruitfulness that God wants you to have and that you can pass on to others. Remember, the hard things in our lives can bring forth the best fruit.

3. Let us remember that our own regrets over the past – the grief which we express over our Absaloms – can give great occasion to the enemy. We need to realise that we must be on our guard all the time and not let the failures of the past – which have been dealt with at the cross – damage the present and the future.

4. David allowed self-indulgence to override his obedience to God's law in taking many wives. Absalom's mother Maacah was the daughter of the king of Geshur (see 2 Sam. 3:3). One wonders how much his mother's pagan influence affected his later actions. We shall see in the next chapter how this indulgence affected David's life and seemed to take the edge off his earlier close following of the Lord. Yet how wonderful is the grace of God, that He still gave David a high place in history, calling him 'a man after my own heart' (Acts 13:22).

Chapter 4

Keep Yourself Fighting Fit

Have you ever stopped to consider why David is called a man after God's own heart? One reason, I believe, is that David was single-eyed in his desire for God: 'One thing I ask of the LORD, this is what I seek: that I may dwell in the house of the LORD all the days of my life, to gaze upon the beauty of the LORD and to seek him in his temple' (Ps. 27:4). And although he failed many times, as we all do, he was also a man who realised the absolute importance of holiness, of 'clean hands and a pure heart' (Ps. 24:4). Have you ever put into words the same desires for your own life – a deep desire for God and a deep concern for holiness of life? As we continue to consider the subject of spiritual warfare, it cannot be emphasised too strongly that without holiness of life we will never be able to stand before the enemy. We will be like the Israelites of old at the battle of Ai, who easily should have won as far as numbers and strength were concerned, but who fled ignominiously before their weaker enemy because there was sin in the camp (see Joshua 7).

Jesus said about Himself, 'the Prince of this world is coming. He has no hold on me' (John 14:30). There was no sin in Jesus of which the devil could accuse Him, nor could he claim any territory in His life. With us this is different, as Satan has made inroads into our lives. But when we come to the cross and receive forgiveness of sin and new life in the Spirit, providing we continue to walk in the Spirit, we have the authority over the enemy, and he cannot touch us. Jesus told His disciples, 'I have given you authority to trample on snakes and scorpions and to overcome all the power of the enemy; nothing will harm you' (Luke 10:19).

What are the things in your life that you would regard as snakes and scorpions? Hurtful things said by other people? Hurtful things done to you by other people? Insecurities in your own life that cause fear and confusion at times? This will be dealt with in more detail in a later chapter. Ask God to reveal them to you, and then face them in the Name of Jesus. Whatever their cause, realise that in Christ they need have no power over you now, as you take authority over them in the Name of Jesus.

I remember one day being in a prayer meeting, and one of the members told us, as she arrived, that for several days she had felt really down about something, and would we pray for her? We did, and the prayer meeting continued. Half way through it, during a time of quietness, this same person whom we had prayed for and who was apparently still feeling 'down', suddenly said out loud, 'I'm not having this any longer!' She didn't say anything more out loud, but she obviously had recognised where the feeling came from and had taken authority over it, and she was released. We could see it in her face and manner, and it made a profound impression on me. I wondered why sometimes I allowed things to go on so long, niggling and upsetting me, when there was a way of dealing with it.

In David's case there were many 'snakes and scorpions' that he overcame, and we will consider these now, and the few sad occasions when he allowed himself to be defeated.

David and the scorpion of Saul's jealousy

Following his victory over Goliath, David entered the service of Saul. One of the first things we read about him is that he was successful in all he did (see 1 Sam. 18:5, 14–15). The Authorised Version translates it as 'David . . . behaved himself wisely.' Scripture tells us that 'The fear of the LORD is the beginning of wisdom' (Prov. 9:10). Already in David's young life he had learned to fear the Lord – that is, his attitude to God was one of awe and reverence – and it had produced godly wisdom and understanding. How we need to seek the Lord ourselves for this godly wisdom and a healthy fear of the Lord. David's wisdom and success was noted and approved by the people of Israel: 'But all Israel and Judah loved David, because he led them in their campaigns' (1 Sam. 18:16). It was also noted by Saul, in whom it produced deep-seated jealousy. When the Lord gives us success in our work for Him, it will always arouse jealousy from the enemy of our souls, and he will seek to throw everything at us, as Saul threw his javelin at David: 'Saul had a spear in his hand and he hurled it, saying to himself, "I'll pin David to the wall." But David eluded him twice' (1 Sam. 18:10–11).

In sharp contrast to David's wisdom and success, we see the evil jealousy of Saul, which he never appeared to deal with and which in the end allowed the entrance into his life of a demonic spirit. Jealousy has been the cause of countless murders and other evils, starting with Cain's jealousy of Abel, which resulted in him being the first murderer. Jealousy caused the downfall of Lucifer, whose desire was to raise his throne above the stars of God and to make himself like the Most High (Isa. 14:13–14). Pride was his downfall, but so also was jealousy, and that jealousy has also been directed at the people of God throughout all generations. Satan hates our worship of God, our obedience to God and our successes for God, and he will try to do everything to stop them. That is why we often feel so attacked and under intense pressure. But we too can elude his darts, as David did.

It would be wise also to look to our own hearts and see where jealousy raises its ugly head, because jealousy unchecked in our hearts will grow like a canker, eating away and robbing us of our joy and peace, rendering us unfruitful in ministry and estranged from fellowship with God. Look what happened to Saul. He had been anointed king by Samuel, the prophet of God, and now the Spirit of God had left him and a demonic spirit had taken over. 'Saul was afraid of David, because the LORD was with David but had left Saul' (1 Sam. 18:12). It all really came about because after a battle the women sang this song: 'Saul has slain his thousands, and David his tens of thousands' (1 Sam. 18:7). That wasn't bad recognition – to have thousands attributed to you – but Saul was not contented with that, because someone else, someone he considered his inferior, had tens of thousands attributed to him.

Does this sound familiar? How many churches have been torn apart by this sort of jealousy? 'I should have been chosen for that job, but that man got it – after all I've done for them!' 'I've always done the flowers at church, and now the vicar has asked someone else!' In Christian ministry there can be a tendency to assess someone else's ministry and check up on how many meetings they have and how it compares with your own schedule. When I found myself falling into this trap I remembered where jealousy came from and who it was who epitomised jealousy, and that very quickly knocked it on the head for me. As jealousy is one of Satan's greatest characteristics, it is one we should run from at all costs, because he can ensnare us more quickly with that than with almost anything else. And what an ensnarement!

The antidote

We see a striking contrast to Saul's jealous and ugly spirit towards David's success in the character of Barnabas in Acts 11:22–26. Barnabas rejoiced to see the grace of God when he was sent to visit the new Christians in Antioch. He already had a ministry among the people, yet because he knew there was someone better fitted to do the job, he laid aside any ambition he may have had and went to Tarsus to look for Paul. For a whole year he ministered under his leadership. He was concerned to further the kingdom of God rather than his own interests.

Oh, that there were more Barnabases in the Church today! Not only those who encourage (his name meant

'Son of Encouragement', and he certainly had a gift for encouraging others), but also those who are prepared to see others preferred before them for the sake of the kingdom of God, and give them all the help and encouragement they need instead of jealous back-biting.

The breaker of promises

Saul's continued jealousy of David prompted him to offer his eldest daughter in marriage, on the understanding that David would fight all his battles for him. His secret hope was that David would be killed by the Philistines, relieving him of the guilt. 'Saul said to David, "Here is my elder daughter Merab. I will give her to you in marriage; only serve me bravely and fight the battles of the LORD." For Saul said to himself, "I will not raise a hand against him. Let the Philistines do that!"' (1 Sam. 18: 17). David's humble spirit caused him to waver, but the events that followed make one realise the insincerity of Saul's offer. 'When the time came for Merab, Saul's daughter, to be given to David, she was given in marriage to Adriel of Meholah' (1 Sam. 18:19).

I received a letter once from a woman who told me that her husband, an unbeliever, had told her that if she would give up her church-going and Bible reading, he would remain with her and their marriage would be saved. She did as he asked, but six months later he left her anyway. In her letter she said, 'I lost my faith and my husband, and now I have nothing.' Often we listen to the lies of the enemy and all his promises – 'God does not love you'; 'Look out for number one if you want to get on in the world'; 'Follow my way and I'll make you rich, happy, successful, popular' – and many other such things, only to discover later to our cost that they were a sham. Satan never keeps his word because he is a liar and a thief and will make promises to us which he never intends to keep, and will seek to rob us of our peace, joy and fellowship with God, and the inheritance that is ours through the cross.

Later Saul gave his daughter Michal to David as his wife, hoping that she would be a snare to him. One wonders if Michal had inherited some of her father's baser characteristics. When she might have entrapped him in shame and embarrassment and thus stopped him worshipping God, David was alert to the snare and dealt with it:

> As the Ark of the LORD was entering the City of David, Michal daughter of Saul watched from a window. And when she saw King David leaping and dancing before the LORD, she despised him in her heart . . .
>
> When David returned home to bless his household, Michal daughter of Saul came out to meet him and said, 'How the king of Israel has distinguished himself today, disrobing in the sight of the slave girls of his servants as any vulgar fellow would.'
>
> David said to Michal, 'It was before the LORD . . . I will become even more undignified than this, and I will be humiliated in my own eyes. But by these slave girls you spoke of, I will be held in honour.'
>
> And Michal daughter of Saul had no children to the day of her death.
>
> (2 Sam. 6:16, 20–23).

Don't be afraid to fan the flame

How the devil delights to pour cold water on the flame of our passion for God. We may feel it is not within our culture to express our devotion to God in certain ways, and we feel justified in our feelings and in condemning others who feel and act differently. Surely the worship of God should transcend culture, and we should be able to accept another's expression of worship, just as we hope that they will accept ours. Poor David. After his wonderful exhilaration at this great moment in Israel's history, when he had brought back the Ark of God to Jerusalem, in the very place where he should have had acceptance and understanding – namely, in his own home – he received the ultimate put-down. Although it must have wounded him deeply, he did counter the attack, not allowing himself to wallow in shame, as Satan would have wished and which so often we allow. 'I'll never do that again. I'll keep my mouth shut from now on,' we say to ourselves, and we retreat into the sulks, thus adding another victory to the enemy.

Watch the critical spirit

Many of us, I am sure, have had feelings like Michal's, and so at this point we will look at a very important feature of David's character which placed him under God's protection and blessing and into which we need to look very carefully today for our own lives. I believe this is a feature which is very much lacking in the Church today, and therefore the door has been left wide open for enemy attack. I am referring to David's refusal to touch the Lord's anointed. In David's case it resulted in him sparing Saul's life several times, even when his advisers urged him to take the opportunity as a gift from God and to rid them and the nation of a bad king. One striking incident occurs in 1 Samuel 24:1–7:

> After Saul returned from pursuing the Philistines, he was told, 'David is in the Desert of En Gedi.' So Saul took three thousand chosen men from all Israel and set out to look for David and his men near the Crags of the Wild Goats.
>
> He came to the sheep pens along the way; a cave was there, and Saul went in to relieve himself. David and his men were far back in the cave. The men said, *'This is the day the LORD spoke of when he said to you, "I will give your enemy into your hands for you to deal with as you wish."'* Then David crept up unnoticed and cut off a corner of Saul's robe.
>
> Afterwards, David was conscience-stricken for having cut off a corner of his robe. He said to his men, 'The LORD forbid that I should do such a thing to my master, the LORD's anointed, or lift my hand against him; *for he is the anointed of the LORD.'* With these words David rebuked his men and did not allow

them to attack Saul. And Saul left the cave and went his way.

(1 Sam. 24:1–7)

David remembered that Saul had been chosen by God to be king. He had been anointed by the prophet Samuel for this purpose, and it was up to God, not David, to remove him.

It is a very sad reflection of our lack of reverence for God today that we constantly criticise those in Christian leadership, thinking we are just being discerning. It has been said that some people have roast clergy for Sunday lunch, and this has been the source of many jokes. But what we are actually doing is undermining the work of God and agreeing with the accuser of the brethren (see Rev. 12:10).

Because of the feeling that our local church 'belongs to us and therefore we have a right to say what we like and what we dislike about it' (an attitude which is especially common among the Christmas and Easter attenders!), many clergy feel they are walking a tightrope, finding it hard to do what they feel would promote church growth and at the same time not upset certain members of their congregation who feel that any departure from what they've always known and done must be wrong! Chairs instead of pews, coffee after the service, a more understandable liturgy – all these things can cause hurt, upset and anger, and the minister is torn between standing his ground if, after prayer, he feels it is right, and losing members of his flock. It is often the small issues that cause the greatest problems, as Satan is a great stirrer of mud, and mud is best stirred in shallow water. Clergy breakdowns are not unknown; perhaps today there are more than ever. Let us ask ourselves how much we are doing to build up or to destroy our own pastor. With a world out there where people are dying without Christ, let us get these things in perspective and realise that some of the issues that have been known to tear churches apart are utterly trivial in the light of eternity.

As we criticise and pull down other members of the body of Christ, not only are we siding with the devil and helping him in his work, but it can also be like cursing someone, and in Chapter 6 we will think about the serious effects of this. Of course, we need to be discerning, and where there is serious biblical error we should warn others who may be led astray. But let us be careful that we only point out the error and do not go on to defame the person's character. We need to attack the problem, not the person. Someone has made the sad but true comment that the Christian Church is the only army which shoots its wounded. What a tragic contrast to the attitude and actions of its Founder!

If other Christian leaders would go in humility and love to the one who is in error to point out the error from the Scriptures and correct them as a brother privately, instead of castigating them in public and ruining even the good aspects of their ministry, I believe we might begin to see the revival and renewing of the Church for which we are all longing and praying. We read in 1 Peter 4:17 that judgment will begin with the family of God – that is, the Church – because God cannot visit and feel at home in a defiled church, as we see so clearly from the book of Revelation. Satan is always directing his attacks against the Church, and very often his most powerful work is done within the Church and not through what comes from the outside. We need to be strongly on our guard against this and to make sure we are not part of the problem.

The danger of being a people-pleaser

Another place where Satan can often trip us up is in our human desire to please people, sometimes at too great a cost. There is the story in 2 Samuel 1 of the Amalekite who lied to David about the death of Saul, hoping that by saying that he had killed Saul, he would gain favour with David, and perhaps have a position in his army. How wrong he was!

'Why were you not afraid to lift your hand to destroy the LORD's anointed?'
     Then David called one of his men and said, 'Go,

strike him down!' So he struck him down, and he died. For David had said to him, 'Your blood be on your own head. Your own mouth testified against you when you said, "I killed the LORD's anointed."'

(2 Sam. 1:14–16)

All for the sake of trying to curry favour! Let us be alert to Satan's wiles, as so often he tries to trip us with the worry, 'What will people think of me?'

And we put pleasing people before pleasing the Lord. 'Fear of man will prove to be a snare, but whoever trusts in the LORD is kept safe.' (Prov. 29:25). Please don't misunderstand me. There is a sense in which it is right to try and please people. Timothy was an example of that. We read in Acts that he had favour with all the people, and I am sure that was partly why Paul took him under his wing – he was a worthy man, by all accounts. But it is the motive that is important. Our first desire should always be to please the Lord. Sometimes that won't fit in with people's wishes – even those of our family members. That is hard, but our first loyalty is to the Lord. After that, the closer we walk with the Lord, the more we will want to do those things that bring pleasure to those we love.

Guard against rebellion

There is a very sobering story in the book of Numbers about the sons of Korah. They were priests who grumbled against the leadership of Moses and Aaron. Jealousy was at the root of this: 'The whole community is holy, every one of them, and the LORD is with them. Why then do you set yourselves above the LORD's assembly?' (Num. 16:3). Under this criticism Moses did exactly what he should have done. He fell down before the Lord and, having told them that God Himself would show who belonged to Him and who was holy (verse 5), he then went on to expose the nature of the problem: 'It is against the LORD that you and all your followers have banded together' (verse 11) – not against Aaron or Moses, but against God. Because God needed His people to be the preservers of His Word and the forbears of the Messiah, such rebellion could not be allowed to go unchecked, and the results of it were devastating. An earthquake killed Korah and his followers (verses 31–34). Others involved in the rebellion were consumed with fire. It should be noted that they were priests who had put fire and incense into their censors, and they were, as far as they were concerned, 'doing the work of the LORD' – and yet they were doing it with unholy hearts and hands. Rebellion against God had taken root in their hearts, and the very thing that should have produced blessing turned out to be a curse for them. (Incense is likened to praise and worship in Rev. 5:8 – 'golden bowls full of incense, which are the prayers of the saints.')

James tells us, 'Submit yourselves, then, to God. Resist the devil, and he will flee from you' (James 4:7). In all aspects of spiritual warfare it is essential that we keep short accounts with God, that we keep our hearts pure before Him. This means having no known and unconfessed sin in our lives, and particularly it means resisting rebellion. We need to remember that in God's sight 'Rebellion is as the sin of witchcraft' (1 Sam. 15:23 AV). So our rebellion against God puts us in league with Satan and all his works. It is one of his major weapons today. The present disrespect for authority and the violence on our streets are symptoms of this problem of rebellion. Therefore, if we are to stand before the enemy 'and having done all, to stand' (Eph. 6:13 AV), we do need to remain under the Lord's protection and cover, and we can remain there only by being in submission to Him.

We saw earlier how David refused to lift his hand against the Lord's anointed. Another important aspect of life for him was his refusal to take revenge.

Seeking revenge can trip us up

In the story of Nabal in 1 Samuel 25 we see David up against a situation that most of us have faced at some time – the sting of ingratitude from someone to whom we have been generous with our time, and perhaps with our money and compassion, and they seem to throw it back in our face. This is what happened to David. When he and his men were in need he sent a message to Nabal, described as a very rich man, reminding him of the fact that when Nabal's servants were working alongside David's servants they were well treated and protected – in fact, gracious hospitality had been shown. Now David asked Nabal if he would do the same thing for them in return. It wasn't too much to ask, and Nabal easily had the resources. But the answer that came back was not only one of refusal but also one of disdain: 'Who is this David? Who is this son of Jesse? . . . Why should I take my bread and water, and the meat I have slaughtered for my shearers, and give it to men coming from who knows where?' Later in history great David's Greater Son was to hear similar words: 'Isn't this the carpenter's son? Isn't his mother's name Mary, and aren't his brothers James, Joseph, Simon and Judas? Aren't all his sisters with us? Where then did this man get all these [miraculous] things? And they took offence at him' (Matt. 13:55–57).

David's response to this was one of anger and revenge: 'It's been useless – all my watching over this fellow's property in the desert so that nothing of his was missing. He has paid me back evil for good. May God deal with David, be it ever so severely, if by morning I leave alive one male of all who belong to him!' Had he gone through with it, the very men whom he had once protected would have been his victims and much innocent blood would have been shed.

In this case it took the intervention of a godly woman, Abigail, to avert this tragedy for the men and for David. She came to him with ample provisions, an abject apology, and deep humility, prepared even to take the blame. 'When Abigail saw David, she quickly got off her donkey and bowed down before David with her face to the ground. She fell at his feet and said: "My lord, let the blame be on me alone"' (1 Sam. 25:23–24). She showed the situation to David as it really was: 'May my lord pay no attention to that wicked man Nabal. He is just like his name – his name is Fool, and folly goes with him' (verse 25). In other words, she was saying, 'David, don't allow this situation – which is really quite trivial because of the person at the centre of it – to get blown out of all proportion and to lead you into sin and to allow the enemy to triumph over you through it.'

Not only did Abigail give the gentle answer that turns away wrath (see Prov. 15:1), but she even had a prophetic gifting and was able to encourage David concerning his future and to show how important it was that he did not sin in this way: 'Please forgive your servant's offence, *for the* LORD *will certainly* make a lasting dynasty for my master, because he fights the LORD's battles. Let no wrongdoing be found in you as long as you live' (1 Sam. 25:28).

'Do not take revenge, my friends, but leave room for God's wrath, for it is written: "It is mine to avenge; I will repay," says the Lord' (Rom. 12:19). David left it to God, and God dealt with Nabal:

> When Abigail went to Nabal, he was in the house holding a banquet like that of a king. He was in high spirits and very drunk. So she told him nothing until daybreak. Then in the morning, when Nabal was sober, his wife told him all these things, and his heart failed him and he became like a stone. About ten days later, the LORD struck Nabal and he died.
>
> (1 Sam. 25:36–8)

Don't get side-tracked

The devil delights to get us side-tracked and away from the real battle, which one day will result in his final downfall. If he can get us off on some skirmish on the sidelines, then he will, and if he succeeds he wins. There are many Christians today who are unable to engage in spiritual warfare for their family, their church, or their town because their lives have been messed up by bitterness and anger over a situation like the one involving David and Nabal. Someone hurt them, or let them down, or showed great ingratitude for past kindnesses, and they have allowed that to take them out of the battle. Their minds and hearts are consumed with self-pity, anger and bitterness, and in their hearts they do what David refused to do.

In the next chapter we will look into the blessing and freedom we receive when we forgive others.

Chapter 5

Our Choices Are Important

The choice to forgive and its results

Bitterness doesn't just affect the person about whom we are bitter, but everyone else around us, and particularly ourselves. In fact, it probably doesn't affect the person we are bitter against at all. They may not even know and possibly wouldn't even care if they did, but it does affect us deeply. That is why the writer to the Hebrews wrote, 'See to it . . . that no bitter root grows up to cause trouble and defile many' (Heb. 12:15).

Sometimes we feel that if we forgive someone who has grossly harmed us we are 'letting them off the hook', and they will get away with it scot-free. It is very important that we do let them off our hook; otherwise we are, as it were, carrying them around with us all the time in our anger and bitterness. When we let them off our hook we are free, and God is able to work, because they are not off His hook, as we saw in the last chapter concerning David and Nabal.

A striking illustration of someone who experienced the freedom and blessing of forgiving another is in the story of the Dutch woman, Corrie ten Boom, following her experience in a Nazi concentration camp. Her father, her brother and her sister had all died under the Nazis, and she had seen her sister mistreated and then die. Later, after the war, she went back to Germany to preach about the love of God. At one of her meetings she recognised the guard who had been the cruellest to her sister. At the end of the meeting he came up to her with an extended hand and said, 'I have now found the Lord and I am asking everyone who has been in a concentration camp to forgive me for what I did. Will you forgive me?' How could she respond to that? She struggled with it for a while, and then, by an act of her will, not her emotions, she put her hand out and said, 'I forgive you.' At that moment she experienced a great freedom. She was free from the bitterness and anger that had been in her life all those years. And we can know this too.

A number of years ago I worked under someone who had caused a lot of hurt to me and others, and I was angry and bitter about this person, who I felt should have known better. It caused me a lot of anguish. I struggled with this for months, and then one day I realised that it was incongruous for me to be teaching people about the love of God and His forgiveness and grace, and at the same time to be harbouring anger and bitterness in my own heart. As I cried out to the Lord, saying, 'I hand over to you my bitterness', I was reminded of the verse, 'be filled with the Spirit' (Eph. 5:18). Of course, the Holy Spirit was in my life, as I was a Christian, but I realised that He was quenched in my life because of the bitterness. I then said to the Lord, 'I accept this [verse] as a command and a promise.' As I asked the Holy Spirit to fill me, in obedience to the command, I knew He would do it, fulfilling the promise. The prayer was prayed, and I continued on into my very busy day. At the end of the day, when I returned home, I became aware of a deep peace and joy which I hadn't known for months, and I was aware that the bitterness had completely gone. I was free. When something is removed from our lives we need at once to be sure that the place is filled by the Holy Spirit, and we do this by asking (Luke 11:13).

Physical wounds heal in time, providing they don't get infected. If infection sets in, the wound cannot heal, and antibiotics must be given, or even surgery may be needed to cut away the dead flesh and to scoop out the infected part. Similarly, our emotional and spiritual wounds will heal providing we do not let them get infected by bitterness. If we do let bitterness in, the wound will only get deeper and more painful. It may be towards a person, about circumstances or against God Himself. But while bitterness is there, healing cannot take place, and Satan can use that bitterness very much to his own ends.

A man after God's own heart

David did not allow himself to get side-tracked by Satan through bitterness about his treatment by Saul or Nabal (although with Nabal he sailed pretty close to the wind), because he realised that whatever he did with a bitter and angry spirit in word or deed, he would actually be doing it against God. A lot of the time, when we say we are angry with this or that person or circumstance, deep in our hearts, we are really angry with God, and if *we* don't realise it, the devil does, and capitalises on it. In his attitude towards Saul, David was truly a man after God's own heart.

Several of the psalms which David wrote show his desire to follow and be close to God and for purity of heart. Psalm 15 is one such example:

> LORD, who may dwell in your sanctuary?
> Who may live on your holy hill?
> He whose walk is blameless
> and who does what is righteous,
> who speaks the truth from his heart
> and has no slander on his tongue,
> who does his neighbour no wrong
> and casts no slur on his fellow-man,
> who despises a vile man
> but honours those who fear the LORD,
> who keeps his oath
> even when it hurts,
> who lends his money without usury [i.e. exorbitant
>   or unlawful interest]
> and does not accept a bribe against the innocent.
> He who does these things
> will never be shaken.

Many times we give Satan authorised access into our lives by not immediately dealing with our sins. The word of gossip, the uncontrolled temper, the enjoyment of pornographic material, the 'harmless' dabbling with horoscopes or fortune tellers (these things are never harmless) and many other such things can all open doors for satanic attack, which usually takes us by surprise. Every time we feel particularly attacked by Satan, we should ask ourselves first, 'Have I done anything to warrant this?' And then we should come before the Lord in repentance if some sin is revealed.

The choice to sin and its results

A very tragic blot on David's life was his sin of adultery with Bathsheba, and then the murder of her husband. Sins like these are not isolated cases. Usually there are signs and symptoms in our lives long before serious sin overtakes us, and we do well to be alert to notice the signs and symptoms and to deal with them before it is too late. I remember that the Principal of the Bible college which I attended warned us students to ask God to show us areas of our lives that could one day cause shipwreck. A very salutary warning.

We read in 2 Samuel 11 that 'In the spring, at the time when kings go off to war, David sent Joab out with the king's men and the whole Israelite army ... *But David remained in Jerusalem*' (verse 1). What caused David to remain in Jerusalem when he should have been out with his troops? How easy it is to make good excuses for our wrongdoing. 'Joab needs the experience and it would be nice for him to have all the honours of success. I'll step out of the picture and let him take all the glory.' How gracious! Or, 'I think I've done enough. Let someone else do the work. I need a rest. Surely I'm due some respite.' All very true and apparently noble. And we've all made such excuses. But in the end we have known, like David, sometimes to our infinite cost, that no excuse will ever make up for not doing what, deep down in our heart, we know to be right.

So David stayed in the comfort of his home and self-indulgence won the day. 'One evening David got up

from his bed and walked around on the roof of the palace'
(2 Sam. 11:2). Was he unable to sleep? Was his conscience
bothering him? If it was, the best thing to do would have
been to go to the Lord in prayer and repentance. But it
seems that David decided that physical exercise was what
was needed and not spiritual examination. How often we
make the same mistake. When we have done wrong we try
our own methods of righting things, instead of going to the
One who is able to help us at every level of our lives.

David, now wide open to temptation, and unaware of his
danger, saw Bathsheba taking her bath, and his desire for
her overcame him. He sent to find out who she was, and
then, hearing that she was the wife of another man, he still
decided to go ahead with his desire for instant gratification.
He would have known that her husband, Uriah, was out
fighting with Joab, and so the timing seemed right!

Satan doesn't have any new tactics and his methods have
always been the same. In Eve's temptation we read that what
she *saw* was *pleasing* and *desirable*, and she *took*. David saw
something pleasing and desirable and he took. The Apostle
John describes the avenues of temptation as the cravings of
sinful man (lust of the flesh), the lust of his eyes and the
boasting of what he has and does (the pride of life), and
all our temptations come through these three avenues (see
1 John 2:15–16).

Jesus was also tempted along these lines, but he resisted.
In Matthew 4 we see him in the wilderness, hungry after
fasting for forty days and nights. There would have been
nothing wrong in making stones into bread, but at whose
command? Then from the highest pinnacle of the Temple
Satan tempted Him to the pride of life by saying, 'Throw
yourself down. You know God will send his angels to protect
you.' To which Jesus replied, 'Do not put the Lord your
God to the test' (Matt. 4:6–7). 'Let's see how far I can go
and still be all right.' How many young people have said
that to themselves over drugs, or illicit sex, and then lived
to regret bitterly their decision to experiment, or worse still,
have died in the attempt.

Finally, having been shown all the kingdoms of the world

and being promised them with a price attached – 'if you will bow down and worship me' (there is always a price attached to sin) – Jesus's reply was, 'Away from me, Satan! For it is written: "Worship the Lord your God, and serve him only"' (Matt 4:9–10). We should note that Jesus's weapons were nothing more than what is available to us in our struggle against temptation – namely, the Word of God and the Spirit of God.

Sadly, unlike the One whom David foreshadowed, he succumbed to his temptation with dreadful consequences. We can often think that our sin is ours alone, and providing we are not caught, all will be well. How often we hear today in our permissive society, 'It's OK as long as it doesn't hurt anyone.' What we need to realise is that sin *always* hurts others beside ourselves, and David's sin was no exception. Bathsheba became pregnant: 'Oh, no! I hadn't bargained for that. A one-night stand, and this happened. It's really not fair!' It never is 'fair' when we are in the wrong!

Then David began to kick over the traces and decided to use his power and authority as the king. He sent for Uriah, ostensibly to hear about the battle. He tried to make him go home, but Uriah refused. 'The ark and Israel and Judah are staying in tents, and my master Joab and my lord's men are camped in the open fields. How could I go to my house to eat and drink and lie with my wife? As surely as you live, I will not do such a thing!' (2 Sam. 11:11). (Did Uriah have an inkling of the truth?) The next night David invited him to dinner and even made him drunk, in the hope of getting him to sleep with his wife and thereby to cover over David's sin. But David, what happened to the blameless heart you wrote about, and weren't you the man who 'does his neighbour no harm'? Oh, David, how indeed are the mighty fallen! Satan certainly gained a victory that day.

But even getting Uriah drunk didn't work, so more violent methods had to be used. David arranged with Joab to have Uriah killed by the enemy. 'Put Uriah in the front line where the fighting is fiercest. Then withdraw from him so that he will be struck down and die' (2 Sam. 11:14) – so said David in a letter to Joab. And this time David's plan worked.

'When Uriah's wife heard that her husband was dead, she mourned for him. After the time of mourning was over, David had her brought to his house, and she became his wife and bore him a son' (verses 26–27).

And no one was any the wiser. And you can imagine the courtiers and friends of Bathsheba thinking how wonderful it was for her, to become the king's wife after the sorrow of her husband's death. 'How wonderful for her, and what a wonderful king we have! So magnanimous! And what a lovely addition to the royal household this beautiful woman will be!' There was just one problem: 'the thing David had done displeased the LORD' (verse 27).

The secret sin revealed

Nathan the prophet came in and told his story of the poor man with the little ewe lamb who was robbed of his treasure by the rich man who had everything. The story was calculated to raise the anger of the usually compassionate David, and it did. And in his anger David pronounced his own sentence: 'David burned with anger against the man and said to Nathan, As surely as the LORD lives, the man who did this deserves to die! He must pay for that lamb four times over, because he did such a thing and had no pity' (2 Sam. 12:5–6). What a shock it must have been when Nathan then pointed at him and said, 'You are the man!' And having reminded him of all the good things which God had done for him and had given him, he then answered David's judgment of the man in the story by pointing out the fourfold punishment that would befall David. The punishment fitted the crime, and first we see that as Uriah died in battle, so the sword would not depart from David's house (verse 10). Then, out of David's own household calamity would come. We saw that in Chapter 3, when we looked at the state of his family and his rebellious sons. Because he had destroyed someone else's home, his home would now be under attack (verse 11).

Then the secret immorality of David and Bathsheba was to result in open shame, as 'Before your very eyes I will take your wives and give them to one who is close to you, and he will lie with your wives in broad daylight. You did it in secret, but I will do this thing in broad daylight before all Israel' (2 Sam. 12:11–12). This was later fulfilled by his son, Absalom. Because David admitted his sin, Nathan told him, 'The LORD has taken away your sin. You are not going to die. But because by doing this *you have made the enemies of the LORD show utter contempt*, the son born to you will die' (2 Sam. 12:13–14).

Sin is costly

We need to recognise that every time we wilfully sin and, as in David's case, do nothing about it, we give the enemies of God occasion to blaspheme and to show contempt – both His human enemies and the principalities and powers. And it is with the latter that we are most concerned in this book. By his sin David gave Satan authorised access in this situation to do his worst in his life. It would have been a year between the sin with Bathsheba and Nathan's appearance at court to challenge David. Was God waiting for him to repent before taking these measures? And yet David kept quiet. Some scholars feel that Psalm 32 may have been written during this time. In it David talks about silence over known sin making him feel like his bones were wasting away and his strength was being sapped. I am sure we can all identify with that from some time in our lives! Psalm 51 is also attributed to this time, and there we see David's deep contrition and repentance, and unlike his predecessor, Saul, and some of us, he makes no excuses. 'For I know my transgressions, and my sin is always before me. Against you, you only, have I sinned and done what is evil in your sight' (Ps. 51:3–4).

So what conclusions can we draw from all of this? First of all, if we are really going to stand against the enemy of our souls and enter fully into Christ's victory, we need to realise that holiness is not an optional extra but an imperative for every believer.

Secondly, we need to be constantly alert to see that the disciplines of our life are not going by the board. Paul said he needed to keep his body in subjection. In 1 Corinthians 9:24–27 he reminds us that we are in a race and in a battle, and that we are not to run aimlessly or to fight 'like a man beating the air'. He encourages us to maintain discipline in our physical life – that is, how we look after our body and use our body – as it is vitally important if we are to fight effectively.

Thirdly, we need to keep our hearts free from rebellion, bitterness and lack of forgiveness.

Lastly and most importantly, we need to keep close to the Lord in prayer, in the study of His Word, and in the fellowship of His Church. We need each other, and sometimes our isolation from the people of God can allow sin to enter unchecked and unnoticed. The writer to the Hebrews, being aware of this danger, wrote, 'See to it, brothers, that none of you has a sinful, unbelieving heart that turns away from the living God. *But encourage one another daily, as long as it is called Today, so that none of you may be hardened by sin's deceitfulness*' (Heb. 3:12–13).

Chapter 6

Battling the Giants of Fear and Insecurity

If we are honest with ourselves, most of us would admit to fears and insecurities in our lives. Now and again, these pitch us into situations or behaviour which we would not choose and which often have disastrous results. Fear of failure can keep us from trying to do something that others see we could do. Then, with hindsight, we regret allowing our fear to overcome right judgment. Deep basic insecurity fostered in childhood can frequently rear its ugly head, and we can feel entrapped and helpless in the situation. Satan knows our weaknesses and will always prey on them, seeking to render us ineffective for the kingdom of God. This need not be so, and we need to take steps to overcome such insecurities.

After an unsuccesful attempt at discipling a young man over several months, Neil Anderson wrote:

> The crux of my interaction with people has been to expose the insidious reality of Satan's relentless assault of deception on the Christian's mind. He knows that if he can keep you from understanding who you are in Christ, he can keep you from experiencing the maturity and freedom which is your inheritance as a child of God . . . Your past has shaped your present belief system and will determine your future unless it is dealt with.[3]

We see some of these thought patterns in the life of David, and we also see how Satan exploited the situations to his own ends.

The Giant Fear

In 1 Samuel 21, after David had heard from his friend Jonathan that Saul really did mean to kill him, and the two friends parted in tears, swearing lifelong allegiance to each other, David went off to Nob, to Ahimelech the priest, in need of sustenance and protection. Ahimelech was fearful when he saw David, and so David lied to him. In today's parlance we would say he was 'economical with the truth'. When Ahimelech asked David why he was alone, David answered that Saul had sent him on a secret mission and that his men were to meet him at a secret location. He then asked for bread and a weapon. The result of this deception David must have regretted to the end of his life. For sustenance he received the consecrated bread and for protection he was given the sword of Goliath. But this resulted in the death of Ahimelech and the eighty-five priests of Nob and all the inhabitants of the town (1 Sam. 22:6–19).

After David was told the tragic outcome of his visit, he admitted, 'That day, when Doeg the Edomite was there, I knew he would be sure to tell Saul' (1 Sam. 22:22). How important it is to listen to the warnings in our hearts! For the Christian the Holy Spirit will often put a check in our heart over something, and we ignore it at our peril. A friend of mine entered into a relationship that later turned out disastrously. When we talked about it later she said that she had seen a number of warning signs beforehand, but she had ignored them all.

Believe God's Word

Another area of our lives where Satan often gains a victory over us is in shaking our confidence in the Word of God. Right at the beginning and across the pages of history we hear the words ringing out, 'Did God really say . . .?' (Gen. 3:1). Even some eminent theologians have fallen prey to that trap! David had been told by Samuel that God had chosen him to be king and had anointed him for that task. Even from Jonathan and Saul he had heard predictions of his kingship (1 Sam. 23:17). But after a long period of being chased by Saul, living in the caves of Adullam with the misfits of society, whom he turned into an effective, well-trained army, and following an outstanding victory over his own baser nature in refusing to kill Saul, he was now attacked by feelings of fear and unbelief. 'But David thought to himself, "One of these days I shall be destroyed by the hand of Saul. The best thing I can do is to escape to the land of the Philistines. Then Saul will give up searching for me anywhere in Israel, and I will slip out of his hand"' (1 Sam. 27:1). Previously fear of the Philistines had caused David to fake madness in front of King Achish (1 Sam. 21:10–15) – what lengths fear will take us to! But now he sought to gain favour with the king, and so began a bleak period in his life – a period of killing and plunder and more deception. To try and gain the trust of the Philistines he pretended he was attacking his own people, and because of this he murdered everyone in every town he took, so that no one could inform on him. As F. B. Meyer put it: 'It was a life of deceit that was wholly unworthy of a servant of the Most High.' It is thought that no psalms were written during this period.

Disappointment and disaster bring David back to God

It is interesting to note that the very thing David had wanted during this period was not achieved by his deceit. When the Philistine army set itself in array against Israel, David had hoped to be trusted enough to go with them. In fact he did set out with them, but the Philistine officers raised such objections that he was told by the king to leave. Maybe they saw through him where the king did not – but it is more likely that in the economy of God David was being saved yet again from himself and from a dangerously false move.

Either he would have faced the awfulness of fighting against his own people and even of killing Saul and

Jonathan, or he may have had it in mind, as the Philistine officers suspected, to turn on his recent friends in the midst of the battle, thus committing another evil to remain with him all his life. At all events, he was saved from both ugly possibilities, and he and his men returned to Ziklag, where they had been living with their families. What horror greeted David and his men on returning home, to find that what they had been doing to others for many months had now happened to them! Their town had been ransacked and burnt by marauding Amalekites and their wives and children had been taken captive. 'When David and his men came to Ziklag, they found it destroyed by fire and their wives and sons and daughters taken captive. So David and his men wept aloud until they had no strength left to weep' (1 Sam. 30:3–4).

Poor David. Not only was he grieving for the loss of his wives and children and those of his men, but now there was talk among them of stoning him, because they laid the blame fully upon him. I wonder if some of them felt pangs of conscience at the wholesale killing and the subsequent deceit, and were angry at the man who had led them into this? What consequences our actions have on others!

But it seems at last as though the awfulness of this situation brought David back to God, as we perhaps have often experienced in our own lives. How sad that God sometimes has to allow desperate situations to enter our lives to bring us to our senses. In verse 6 we read those lovely and challenging words, 'But David found strength in the LORD his God' (verse 6). Or as the Authorised Version puts it, 'David encouraged himself in the LORD his God.' Do we do this in times of crisis? And having done that, David once again began to seek God for guidance, resulting in the successful recovery of all the property and families of David and his men, and the recovery of David's compassion and sense of justice. Some of the men who had been too exhausted to go on were to be denied the spoils of recovery. If 'the evil men and troublemakers among David's followers' (verse 22) had had their way, those who had stayed behind would have been given their wives and children only.

But David intervened with, 'No, my brothers, you must not do that with what the LORD has given us . . . The share of the man who stayed with the supplies is to be the same as that of him who went down to the battle. All shall share alike' (1 Sam. 30:23–24). David was really back on course again with the Lord. 'David made this a statute and ordinance for Israel from that day to this' (verse 25). And an important spiritual principle is seen here too: that those who stay at home and are prayer warriors will be rewarded as much as those in the front line on the mission field for whom they have prayed.

Shore up your weak points

Satan will always attack our weakest point, so it is important to know what that point is. If possible we should find out how it came into being – perhaps through some childhood experience or an inherited characteristic. Then we should deal with it by bringing it to the Lord, acknowledging the problem, repenting if necessary, and then realising that in Christ there are no insecurities that cannot be dealt with.

What will people think?!

Desire for acceptance and fear of rejection are real issues for all of us. Satan often uses them to try and intimidate us. For example, I have often had great feelings of insecurity about what I should wear on certain occasions. Prior to speaking at meetings and conferences, I would often get into quite a state worrying about my clothes. This was partly due to the fact that whenever I told my mother that I had spoken at a meeting or had been somewhere special, her first question was always 'What did you wear?' It became a very important issue to me, as it had been to her. Sometimes it was clear to me what I should wear, and then I would go off in peace and enjoyment. At other times, if I dithered and changed my mind, I would go off conscious of myself and full of uncertainty, often feeling when I got to the meeting that I was wearing the wrong outfit, and then I would really have a battle on my hands before getting up to speak. I had to face up to the fact that this was really pride, although I think it's important for Christians to look nice and reasonably fashion-conscious. I think we have been rightly criticised for failure in this in the past. What was important was for me to be appropriately dressed, well prepared in heart and mind, and then to go to the meeting with my mind on the people to whom I would speak, and to know what the Lord was wanting to say to them.

Of course, the enemy will do all he can to distract my mind, especially from prayer, because he knows how vitally important prayer is. Even if we do not realise it, Satan is very conscious of the power of prayer, and he will do everything he can to get our minds and hearts off that and on to ourselves, so that we don't have the time or the inclination to pray, or we may not even think about it, because we are so busy worrying about relatively unimportant issues.

On a much more serious level, if a child has grown up being told it is no good at anything, stupid, clumsy, not wanted, wicked and so forth, the child will believe it: 'It must be true if Mum and Dad say so.' But is it? And those thoughts are embedded in the conscious mind and then in the subconscious, where they stay and can exert influence throughout adult life.

It is no good saying, 'I'll try not to think that way any more.' It doesn't work. I am sure we've all found that. These thoughts of error need to be replaced by thoughts of truth. Neil Anderson points out in his book that our struggle against Satan is a truth struggle, not a power struggle. We need to out-truth him with the Word of God.

Know who you are in Christ

Who are you? As a Christian you are a child of God, beloved of God, chosen of God, called to a life of fruitfulness and good works, called to fullness of life, cleansed and redeemed and clothed in the righteousness of Christ, and 'blessed . . . with every spiritual blessing in Christ' (Eph. 1:3). Where should our insecurities be now? Finished and done away with. I know it sounds 'easier said than done', and we all struggle with this, and sometimes Satan revives memories in us that we thought were long gone. As we take the Word of God and *believe* it and rely on it, we can see our insecurities go. For some reason I had a lot of insecurities as a child, as a teenager, as a young adult and on into older years. But I have found as I have allowed the Holy Spirit to have greater control of me, He has graciously and gently shown me things in my life, some from the past, that He has then healed. Also, as I have come to a greater awareness of my position in Christ, I have found a confidence I never had before.

David was a man who had insecurities and fears, as we have seen, and yet he was able confidently to say, 'The LORD is my light and my salvation – whom shall I fear? The LORD is the stronghold of my life – of whom shall I be afraid? . . . Though my father and mother forsake me, the LORD will receive me . . . Wait for the LORD; be strong and take heart and wait for the LORD' (Ps. 27:1, 10, 14). It is vital in our fight against the enemy that we know who we are in Christ and that we know the authority He has given us.

Guard the door of your heart

Sometimes I view my life like a fortress, and when the enemy is besieging me I need to be careful not to open the door even half an inch, because he will burst in at the sign of the least crack. Opening the door to fear is an example of this. When I was diagnosed as having breast cancer fear rushed in and all sorts of imaginations took over. As a friend said to me, 'If that was me, I would have myself dead and buried in my mind by now!' And that's just it. Fear brings its own imagination. After some spiritual warfare prayer with one particularly anointed friend in this type of ministry, the fear went and I decided that the 'door' must be kept firmly closed against further onslaughts. And it was, but this was not always easily done, and certainly only through the Word of God.

Fear, anger (of the wrong sort – not all anger is wrong), thoughts of worthlessness and constant self-blame should be recognised as the enemy's work and dealt with immediately. Like David taking hold of the lion or the bear by its hair when it turned to attack him, we need to realise that often after blessing, or before it, attacks come. We need to be ready for them and to give them no place in our lives or thoughts, and we should deal with them at once: 'I'm not accepting this! *Out!*' The moment we let Satan in, even by a toe, he's in with all the fears and accusations and everything he wants to throw at us, and it's a fight to get him out. I am not talking about satanic possession – of course not – but I am talking about how he can control our thought-patterns and bring us into bondage.

What a contrast to our beautiful Saviour, who meekly says, 'Here I am! I stand at the door and knock. If anyone hears my voice and opens the door, I will come in and eat with him, and he with me' (Rev. 3:20). He knocks gently and waits to be invited, while Satan hammers at our door, demanding to be let in, and the moment the door is opened a crack he bursts his way in and settles. Jesus comes graciously in, waiting to be invited to every room.

Someone once said, amusingly but with much truth, 'If you invite the devil for tea he'll bring his pyjamas.' *Don't give him the opportunity*. Guard the house of your life as carefully as you would guard your home. How saddened we are when we hear of the elderly who allow the wrong people to come into their homes and then find they have been robbed of their life savings. Many of us Christians do that spiritually all the time and find ourselves robbed of joy, peace and fruitfulness. Even though for us these things may be only a temporary setback, I believe that as we grow in Christian maturity we should seek to have this happen less and less.

Many Christians, myself included, have allowed Satan to rob them of their joy, peace and usefulness by indulging in self-condemnation, when the *fact* is that 'there is now no condemnation for those who are in Christ Jesus' (Rom. 8:1) and that 'the blood of Jesus, his [God's] Son, purifies us from *all* sin' (1 John 1:7). We saw in the previous chapter that we can have freedom and blessing by forgiving others. Some of us find this especially hard because we have never learned to forgive ourselves, and through this we allow Satan to rob us of the blessings that are ours. If God has forgiven me – and He did when I acknowledged my sin and asked for forgiveness by the blood of the cross – then what right have I not to forgive myself? I observed early on in my Christian life that a victorious Christian is not one who doesn't sin, but one who, having sinned, repents quickly, accepts God's forgiveness and goes on, refusing to allow the mistakes of the past to mar the opportunities of the present.

That's not always easy to live up to, because Satan delights to have us wallow in our sins and mistakes and to make us feel we should suffer for them endlessly. I am not in any way saying that repentance is easy – real repentance will be accompanied often by tears and anguish of heart – but once we have truly repented and the Lord has forgiven us, we should again experience the peace and joy of our wonderful Lord, and an even deeper love for Him. So when Satan comes with his taunts we need to protect ourselves with the Word of God to counter him.

Know what your special insecurities are, and face up to them – knowing their origin does help, and God can show you this – and then ask God to help you deal with them so that you can shore up those gaps in the fortress of your life which let the enemy in.

God said to Cain, 'sin is crouching at your door; it desires to have you, but you must master it' (Gen. 4:7). This could also be said of our insecurities. Man was created to have dominion over the earth and all that was in it, and control over our own bodies in discipline. That is why God waits for us to call into being that which He has planned, and that is why Jesus gave authority to us, so that whatever we bind on earth is bound in heaven and whatever we loose on earth is loosed in heaven. Man was made to have dominion – we were created to conquer. Having disobeyed God and obeyed Satan, we have handed over our rights to him, and he is now the prince of this world (John 14:30), and the battle is on. God has allowed him to remain even after the cross to enable us to learn obedience and to exercise this God-given mandate to have dominion over overselves and our passions and over Satan. And God uses even the attacks of the enemy on our lives to make us more godly and usable. The attacks show up our weaknesses, so that we can deal with them.

The classic example of this is Peter and his denial. Why did Jesus give Satan permission to sift Peter like wheat? Peter, the bragger – who had said, 'I will die with you even though others may run away' – had to learn that until his pride was broken he would not be much use in the kingdom of God. When it was broken, after his denial, he was commissioned to feed the flock of God, and after the Day of Pentecost he became the shepherd and leader of the Early Church. So Satan was allowed to sift him, not to destroy him but to accomplish the purpose of God in fitting him for His service. And we continue to see this in the life of David.

Chapter 7

Refusing the Works of Darkness

Some years ago, when I was teaching in a Bible school, a married student told me that her husband was very ill and the doctors were unable to find out what was wrong with him. They had been in Africa as missionaries and she felt that the cause of her husband's illness was that he had been cursed. My reaction at that time was to completely dismiss the whole idea, and I chided her for allowing herself as a Christian to think such thoughts, reminding her of Christ's victory on the cross over the works of Satan, and that as Christians she and her husband were protected. I would not answer her in the same way today, and I regret any hurt I may have caused her. I do not mean by that that I have changed my views about Christ's victory on the cross or the protection of His people – absolutely not! But I do believe that it is possible for curses to affect us and that sins from past generations, as well as some of our own earlier sins, like involvement with the occult, can dog our footsteps until we have them dealt with. This is the subject of this chapter.

Curses

We read in 2 Samuel 16 that when David left Jerusalem and fled from his son Absalom, Shimei, from Saul's clan, came out and cursed David and threw stones at him. His cursing and accusation had some truth in it: 'Get out, get out, you man of blood, you scoundrel! The LORD has repaid you for all the blood you shed in the household of Saul, in whose place you have reigned. The LORD has handed the kingdom over to your son Absalom. You have come to ruin because you are a man of blood!' (2 Sam. 16:7–8). He was a man of blood. That was why God did not have him build the Temple but left it to his son Solomon, the man of peace.

When Satan accuses us there is always some truth in the accusation – otherwise there would be no point in it. But many of us get stuck on that one point of truth, agree with it and go under, instead of admitting it and letting God use the accusation to refine and strengthen us. David recognised the truth behind that cursing and accusation – God had allowed it. I think we should always remember that nothing comes to us except by God's permission, and sometimes these things are allowed just to strengthen us and bring us into closer dependency on God.

However, we do need to make the fine distinction here between the accusation, which can be used to refine us, and a curse from which we need to seek refuge in God, as David did. A curse is words or actions imbued with evil power with the intention of destruction. Sometimes parents, for example, can say things in anger like, 'You'll never be any good' or 'I wish you had never been born.' If the parents at other times show loving concern, words like this would not be a curse, although they can cause some damage. But sometimes these words have been said with real feeling and have been followed up by behaviour that would back up the statement. This then can be a curse, and this should be broken, and we shall see how later.

We have a choice

Satan will always try to destroy us, our ministry and our relationship with God, and it is up to us whether or not that happens. God has given ample provision for our victory over this. If we allow an attack on us to push us into a closer relationship with God and we do not allow ourselves to be driven away in fear, then Satan is defeated. He nearly always oversteps the mark, as we have often seen in the persecution of the Church. How true is the statement, 'The blood of the martyrs is the seed of the Church.' When Satan has tried to destroy the Church through persecution he has only succeeded in strengthening and enlarging it. The Church in China is a great modern-day example of that.

But today, with the rise of witchcraft and the occult in this country, it is good sense to take these things seriously and to know that it is indeed possible for people to be cursed and to feel the effect.

A couple who had been in Christian work for several years had a serious disagreement with a colleague. Before they left the organisation they were told, 'You will never have a ministry again.' That acted as a curse, and for many years they felt the effect of it in their lives and ministry.

How can one deal with a situation like that? It would be important first to take the matter to the Lord, not in anger with the person – remember that Jesus said, 'bless them that curse you' (Matt. 5:44 AV) – but in humility and openness to the Lord. Maybe the curse is totally undeserved – then it will not stick. Proverbs 26:2 tells us that 'Like a fluttering sparrow or a darting swallow, an undeserved curse does not come to rest.' But very often it finds a cause in us, and then repentance is necessary. Ask the Lord if there is something that you do need to repent over in the situation. As He shows you, do it at once. Then, having done that, ask the Lord to remove the curse and give you His blessing. In the case of the couple mentioned, it would be to ask for and claim fruitfulness and blessing and freedom from the curse.

Sometimes it may be necessary and helpful to ask a trusted friend or minister who is familiar with these things to pray with you to cut you off from any effect the curse may have, using perhaps the words given on page 87. But your own attitude to God and any repentance that is necessary is vitally important.

For those engaged in strategic-level spiritual warfare – praying for towns and cities – or in other types of Christian ministry that is being effective, attacks can be expected, and we should be alert to them. This should not be based on fear;

it's just good sense. We can almost take it as a compliment that Satan thinks our ministry is worth attacking.

After a ten-week course in Spiritual Warfare attended by nearly 300 members from 149 churches in one local area, it was noted that in many parts of the town 'taping' had been done around churches and in other parts of the town as well. Taping is an activity of satanic groups who record curses on to a cassette, remove the tape and drape it around lamp-posts or church doors. If you find a tape like this, as I did around a church near where I live, pick it up and destroy it. Then pray for the protection of the people for whom it was meant and for the removal of the curse.

I remember reading once about a Christian couple who began having rows that were quite out of character for both of them. They couldn't understand why this was happening, until someone pointed out the tape on a telegraph wire near their home. Somehow it was removed and destroyed, and the desire and inclination to row left them.

Sometimes you hear people say – and maybe you've said it yourself in a moment of angry frustration or depression – 'I wish I was dead.' There is only one person who will put that thought into your head, and you don't want to listen to him or speak at his command. It is a form of curse on yourself and should be avoided at all costs. If you do say it, ask God's forgiveness at once and proclaim, 'I will not die but live, and will proclaim what the LORD has done' (Ps. 118:17). Please note the two 'wills'. 'I *will* not die (I choose life), and I *will* proclaim . . .' We do have a choice between life and death, blessing or cursing. Deuteronomy 28 very clearly sets this out for us.

Childhood traumas

Much lesser things than those already described can become a curse to us. As previously mentioned, the parent who always tells their child that he or she is stupid, ugly, unwanted or whatever is in a way cursing that child, and the effect is the same. A person can curse parts of their body – 'I hate my arms, my legs, my body' – and then they

wonder why there are problems there. To reverse that, thank
God for that specific part of your body and praise God for
making you as you are.

Sometimes childhood experiences can act like a curse on
us, and we may need to seek out help for deliverance. For
example, a woman who has been sexually abused by a family
member can carry a tremendous sense of guilt, although she
was in no way to blame. After I had spoken at a conference,
a young woman told me that she had been the victim of incest
and had felt dirty all her life as a result. Together we looked
at Zechariah 3, that amazing story of Joshua the high priest
standing before the Lord in filthy robes and Satan standing
at his side accusing him. Did the Lord join in the accusation?
No! 'The LORD said to Satan, "The LORD rebuke you, Satan!
. . . Is not this man a burning stick snatched from the fire?"'
(Zech. 3:2). His garments were then exchanged for clean
ones and a clean turban was put on his head (the seat of
thought and imagination!). 'Then he said to Joshua, "See,
I have taken away your sin, and I will put rich garments
on you"' (verse 4). As she realised that she was clothed in
clean garments, as now she had come to Christ, and that
even the sense of guilt had been taken on the cross, there
was a great feeling of relief and freedom.

Another woman I spoke to with a similar background still
felt the burden of this, but for a different reason. Although
she felt she had forgiven her father, she still did not feel free.
As we talked on I realised that although she may have gone
through the motions of forgiveness, there was still a lot of
anger there, and she admitted that this was so. While anger
or lack of forgiveness is there Satan has a foothold with
us. Jesus tells us in Matthew 6:15 that if we do not forgive
others when they sin against us, we will not be forgiven our
sins. Satan will therefore constantly remind us of the awful
experience, causing us to relive the pain of it time and time
again. We need to rid ourselves of his hold by forgiveness.
By an act of the will we must let go of our bitterness at the
foot of the cross.

In Roman times a convicted murderer had the victim's
body strapped to theirs, and they carried it around until

the rotting flesh caused the death of the convicted man. A gruesome picture! But sadly, there are many people carrying similar awful burdens today, and the only way to freedom is by allowing it to fall off at the foot of the cross and to roll into the empty tomb, like Christian's burden in *Pilgrim's Progress*. This can be done by acknowledgment of the problem – tell it like it is – to God, repentance over bitterness or lack of forgiveness, and renouncing any thoughts of bitterness or revenge. Then ask the Lord to heal, cleanse and free you from any false guilt and from the bitter memories of the past. It is important also to take some portion of the Word of God and proclaim it and claim it over this situation. For example, David's Psalm 145, which begins with a strong declaration of his will and goes on to speak of the love and compassion and power of God, is a wonderful psalm to meditate on and memorise during this time. And there are many other such passages.

The Word of God should always be our weapon in spiritual warfare, and we cannot be without it. I remember reading of a missionary family in the Far East who, soon after they were settled in their new home, found their little boy was waking at night screaming with nightmares. They could not understand this, as it had not happened before they left their homeland. One day someone told them that the house they were currently living in had been owned by a witch-doctor, and all sorts of evil things had taken place there. So the little boy's father went into every room reading the Scriptures aloud and praying, and from that night on there were no more nightmares. This is a very good practice for anyone moving into a new home. You don't know what has taken place there before, and as a Christian you will, I am sure, want to think of your home as being dedicated to the service of God. So go round each room reading God's Word and praying a prayer of dedication. You can also anoint the door posts with oil as a mark of dedication. (See Appendix I.)

This is not fanciful or just for people who live abroad. I heard of a couple who moved into a home here in England, and soon after their arrival the wife woke up in the middle of the night terrified, and she heard herself saying the name of Jesus over and over again. At the same time her husband, lying by her side, had the experience of feeling his spirit leave his body, and he looked down on himself from above. The next morning, when they shared these experiences with each other, they were rightly alarmed and went to speak to their pastor. He advised them first to find out from the estate agents who had lived there before them, and then he promised to come and pray with them. On enquiry they found that a spiritualist medium had lived there and had frequently conducted seances in the bedroom. The pastor came and prayed in the house and particularly in that room, cleansing it. He then asked the man what he had done in his life to allow Satan to have that amount of control over him. The man acknowledged that previously he had been involved with the occult. After repentance of this and prayer he too was set free.

Remembering the Proverbs 26:2 verse about the unde-served curse not coming to rest, the more we seek to live righteously and to keep short accounts with God, the less we are prone to this sort of attack. We also need to remember the Lord's injunction to bless those who curse you, because as we do this we can return the curse from whence it came.

Generational cursing and sin

It seems that some families have problems that go through the generations, and certain patterns seem to emerge. Some families have a history of miscarriages, early deaths, financial problems and many such things. It is helpful to look back into the family tree to see where such things began and what the underlying cause might be.

In 2 Samuel 21 we read the intriguing story of David and the Gibeonites. There was a three-year famine in progress and David did the right and proper thing and prayed earnestly to know the mind of God in this matter. The answer came back that it was because of something Saul had done some years previously in breaking his nation's promise of safety to the Gibeonites. As a result many of them were killed and they were left stateless. Again we might read into this, 'But the thing he had done displeased the LORD', and so famine resulted. But, you might think, surely that was years ago. Saul was now dead, and a good king was in his place. Surely that was all over now. The things that we do can very much affect succeeding generations, and so too can the things that we say. Curses can be handed down from one generation to another, and sin that is not dealt with can affect later generations. Grandparents or great-grandparents who perhaps practised witchcraft or were involved in occult practices can have a profound effect on their grandchildren and great-grandchildren, even though they may never have met. However, it is important to say that we are never condemned for the actions of our ancestors. They have to carry their own responsibility before God, but we can still be spiritually and emotionally affected by their deeds.

Freemasonry is one area that should be mentioned in this connection. Many books have been written on the subject of Freemasonry, so there is now less secrecy about it. But the higher the degree a man reaches, the more he is introduced to the occult, usually without realising it. Churches that are experiencing lack of blessing and difficulties among their people are often ones where there is Freemasonry among the leadership.

On one occasion, when I had mentioned Freemasonry during a talk on Spiritual Warfare, a young woman approached me afterwards to say that her father had been in a high position in the Masons. For years she had felt as though she had a tight hood around her head, until the day her father died. Then it went completely from her and she felt free. She had discovered later that part of her father's regalia was the wearing of a hood. If you have or have had Freemasonry in your family, tell God you renounce it as a false god, and ask Him to completely cut you off from it (Lev. 26:40ff.).

Sometimes it might be helpful to do this with someone else praying for you as well to cut you off, and speaking out loud the declaration on pages 87 and 88. This is also important if you have in any way or at any time been involved in the occult, such as going to a fortune teller (very often we say it was 'Just for fun' without realising its seriousness).

While I was speaking at a Bible conference a young woman came to me and confessed that although she was a Christian, whenever she read the Scriptures, which she did daily out of duty, it seemed dry to her and she got nothing from it. Likewise with prayer. After hearing her out, while quietly praying for guidance in this matter, I asked her if she could think of any reason for this situation. After a short pause she said, 'Before I was a Christian I did get involved in the occult, and my father was a Freemason.' I was very interested that both these things came to her mind without any prompting from me!

I asked her if she had destroyed all her occult books and objects, and she had. I then asked her if she truly repented of her occult involvement, and she assured me that she did (I would usually get someone to pray a prayer of repentance aloud). Then I prayed for her, cutting her off from the occult influence and the influence of her father's Freemasonry. We then talked about her getting more out of the Bible and some practical ways of doing this. It would have been no good at all to do this before the prayer, as the block would still have been there. The next day she came back to see me again. Her face was radiant, and she told me she had spent hours reading the Bible and praying, and everything had come alive to her.

In the case of David and the Gibeonites, this sin was dealt with by the death of seven of Saul's sons. It seems rather a drastic measure, but it was a serious violation of a treaty made by Joshua to the Gibeonites. Joshua and the leaders had sworn on oath to them by the Lord God of Israel that they would live in peace with them forever (Joshua 9:18). Even though this treaty came about as the result of deception, and they were found out, Joshua and his men rightly refused to violate the treaty. Not so Saul, who had massacred many of the Gibeonites, thus violating the treaty. This was a serious offence involving the whole nation in perjury, and it brought God's judgment.

As Saul was no longer alive to atone for this, his remaining family were held responsible. Blood was to be shed to appease the breaking of this binding treaty, which had resulted in the shedding of the Gibeonites' blood. We read that after the death of Saul's sons at the hands of the Gibeonites, 'God answered prayer on behalf of the land' (2 Sam. 21:14). God made known to the children of Israel that the shedding of blood was necessary for forgiveness of sin (see Lev. 17:11). In the Old Testament this was done through animal sacrifices, or in this case a life for a life. This was all a foreshadowing of the One who would give His life-blood for the sins of the world – the supreme and complete sacrifice for all time. So now, through the blood of the cross, we have this victory, but it must be appropriated.

If you feel there are unexplainable difficulties in your family or if you know of occult involvement of any sort, perhaps you would like to consider making the following declaration. Read it through first, to make sure you are in total agreement with it, and then speak it out aloud, preferably before someone else who would pray with you about it:

I bind unto myself the strong name of the Trinity – the Father, the Son and the Holy Spirit. I proclaim Jesus Christ as the Son of God and declare that He came in the flesh. I confess Jesus Christ as my Saviour and Lord and in the Name of Jesus I confess and renounce, repudiate and reverse each and every vow, pact, covenant [obviously our covenant with God is not meant here, but any covenant with another power] and agreement made by myself, or any other member of my family or ancestors, at any time, in any place, with whatsoever person, society or power, and for whatever reason. I especially renounce . . . [any specific renunciation here, e.g. the occult, Freemasonry etc.].

In the Name of Jesus I say to all who hear that I now choose to set myself beneath the everlasting covenant of God, sealed with the precious blood of Jesus.

This covenant annuls, invalidates and countermands all other covenants, and in the Name of Jesus, who was made a curse for me, I renounce and repudiate each and every curse against myself and any other member of my family or ancestors.

In the Name of Jesus I bind and smash the power of any curses and choose to be loosed and stand free from all their negative and detrimental influences, in the Name of Jesus Christ my Lord. Amen, so be it.

Glanville Martin

Generational blessing

It should be mentioned that there is also such a thing as generational blessing, which can have a profound effect on families for good. While writing this chapter a friend told me that her husband's great-grandfather had written into his will a statement concerning his allegiance to Jesus Christ, and how he prayed for all his family and the generations to come that they would follow the Lord. And as a result this had happened. All the children were following the Lord, and she reminded me of this verse in the Psalms: 'from everlasting to everlasting the LORD's love is with those who fear him, and his righteousness with their children's children' (Ps. 103: 17).

Sometimes our problems can come not from generational sin but from what we have allowed to come into our lives and into our homes and around our necks. On another occasion when speaking on Spiritual Warfare, I noticed a lady wearing the key of life. It is a cross with a ring at the top. I hesitated as to whether or not I should say something to her, and then plucked up courage and spoke. She had her coat on by now, so I began by asking her what it was that she was wearing around her neck. I really needed to know if she knew what it was, as many people don't. 'It's the key of life,' she replied. 'I bought it in Egypt.' 'That's right,' I said. 'It's an Egyptian artefact used in fertility rites and in satanic rituals.' As I told her that she looked shocked. Her friend joined her at that point and I left them in conversation. Later that day, over a cup of tea with the committee who had organised the day, the friend asked me what we had been talking about, and I told her. She seemed upset that I had said anything to this lady because, she explained, she was a new Christian and her husband was desperately ill, and they had all sorts of problems in the home. I was not surprised and, although I felt sorry for the poor lady in her problems, at the same time I felt relieved that I had spoken to her, in view of her situation. From what she had told me it sounded as though she had a number of such artefacts in her home and, like the statue in my childhood home that had affected my father, she would have done well to clear them all away and seek cleansing of the house.

I am including at the end of this chapter a list of signs and symbols as well as occult practices to be avoided, and strategic dates in the satanic calendar against which we can be praying.

One final thing which is worthy of mention, because it is very prevalent today, is the story which comes at the end of the life of Saul and is such a sharp contrast to David.

I refer to the sad story, recorded in 1 Samuel 28, of Saul's final downfall when, unable to hear the voice of God for guidance over his battle with the Philistines, he felt the only thing to do was to get supernatural help from a medium, and so he went to the witch of Endor. The medium called up Samuel. It has been suggested that this is the only time that the actual person has been called up (otherwise it is always demonic impersonation), and the damning message of rejection and death which was given would in itself have been enough to show Saul the displeasure of God. This is something that from the beginning was condemned by God: 'Do not turn to mediums or seek out spiritists, for you will be defiled by them. I am the LORD your God' (Lev. 19:31).

How many people today have been caught out with desiring to hear their dead relative, believing that the voice they heard really was their husband or wife, and then have felt entrapped by something they did not understand or want. Much later in history, after Saul's death, God was to tell us through Isaiah, 'When men tell you to consult mediums and spiritists, who whisper and mutter, should not a people enquire of their God? Why consult the dead on behalf of the living?' (Isa. 8:19).

We can be free from all these things if we choose to be, and take the appropriate steps to free ourselves from anything that might have defiled us in the ways mentioned. Let us remember that 'Christ redeemed us from the curse of the law by becoming a curse for us, for it is written: "Cursed is everyone who is hung on a tree." He redeemed us in order that the blessing given to Abraham might come to the Gentiles through Christ Jesus, so that by faith we might receive the promise of the Spirit' (Gal. 3:13–14). So I can say that through the sacrifice of Jesus on the cross I have passed out from under the curse and have entered into the blessing of Abraham, whom God blessed in all things.

Checklist of occult activities

Involvement in any of the following can dangerous:

Witchcraft
White magic or black magic
Necromancy (prediction by communication with the dead)
Fortune-telling by palmistry or crystal ball
Cartomancy, including tarot cards
Numerology – divination using numbers associated with
    a person's name and birthdate
Astrology
Horoscopes
Divination by rod, pendulum or motor skopua (a
    mechanical pendulum for diagnosing illness)
Lithomancy – divination by precious stones or
    coloured beads
Spiritism
Psychic healing
Concept therapy
Hypnosis

Yoga
Transcendental Meditation (T.M.)
Eastern meditation
Ouija boards
Planchette (glasses on table)
Clairvoyance
Extra sensory perception (ESP)
Mental telepathy
Mind dynamics (Silva Mind Control)
Automatic spirit writing
Levitation
Table tapping, spirit knocking or rappings
Parakinesis (PK) control of objects by power of
  mind and will
Martial arts such as Kung-fu, karate, aikido, judo
Heavy acid rock music (e.g. Santana, Black Sabbath)
Hallucinogenic drugs (LSD, heroin, marijuana)
Glue-sniffing
Fantasy role-play games, e.g. 'Dungeons and Dragons'
Occult literature (possession or use is dangerous;
  it should be burned – Acts 19:19)

Amulets, zodiac charms and pagan symbols such as the
ankh (used in satanic rituals) and pagan religious objects,
relics and artefacts should also be disposed of, preferably
by burning.

'When the enemy shall come in like a flood, the Spirit of the
LORD will lift up a standard against him and put him to flight'
(Isa 59:19).

Occult dates

There are certain dates which occultists consider of special
significance. At these times certain rituals are expected
to be performed in tribute to demons and/or gods being
worshipped or called up.

1 January (traditionally a Druid feast day)

20 January (St Agnes Eve)

2 February (candlemas, a witches' sabbat)

Shrovetide (three days before Ash Wednesday, witches' sabbat)

24 April (St Mark's Eve)

30 April (Walpurgis Night, eve of Mayday, a major sabbat)

1 May (Beltane – Celtic pre-Christian spring festival; one of the major witches' sabbats)

23 June (St John's Eve, mid-summer, summer solstice – the most important time for the practice of magic)

25 July (St James' Day)

1 August (Lammas – the Great Sabbat)

24 August (St Bartholomew's Day, Great Sabbat and fire festival)

31 October (Hallowe'en – the dead supposedly return to earth, major festival)

21 December (St Thomas' Day – winter solstice)

Other significant nights are those with a full moon, and at Easter and Christmas gatherings take place for the purpose of mocking Christianity's holiest days.

Occult signs and symbols

Just as there are universally recognisable Christian signs, such as the cross, dove and fish, so has the occult its own symbols. You might see them as graffiti, or in children's notebooks, or even as ink 'tattoos'. If the latter, these may indicate 'dabbling', or in some cases, more serious involvement with the occult.

There is specific occult significance in tattoos/ink markings of: crescent moon with stars of Lucifer, black panthers, goat's head, coiled snake, skull, dragon, crossed bones, spider, black rose, knife dripping blood, horned hand (satanic greeting or salute), or some sexually perverted symbol.

The following are the most commonly used, but by no means include every sign.

Pentagram
The five-pointed star is an important symbol in magic representing the
four elements surrounded by the spirit
and most commonly used by 'white
witches'.

Inverted pentagram
The five-pointed star inverted is associated with black magic and satanism. It
symbolises the goat head which repre-
sents Satan.

Hexagram
Also known as the Star of David or
Crest of Solomon. It was used by the
Egyptians long before Israel adopted
it. It began to be used during the
Babylonian captivity and is today seen
on the Israeli flag. However when used
by occultists it is believed to have
great power.

Cross of Nero:
The Crow's Foot or Broken Cross
(inverted). This was the 'peace' symbol of the '60s but today is being
used by some heavy metal fans and
occultists to represent the defeat of
Christianity.

Swastika
or Sun Wheel; it was an ancient religious
symbol long before Hitler adopted it
and it was used in sun worship. Now it
is a modern symbol of evil. Nazis used it
counter-clockwise to depict movement
away from the Godhead.

Anarchy
Denial of authority. Many adolescents use it to show contempt. It can often be seen at scenes of vandalism where spray-painted satanic graffiti appears on buildings.

Thaumaturgic triangle
Used for magical purposes such as spell casting or demon-summoning.

Udjat
All-seeing eye, sometimes called 'eye of Horus'.

Scarab
Design based on the dung beetle, this is an ancient Egyptian symbol of re-incarnation. It is also associated with Beelzebub, Lord of the Flies.

Lightening bolts
Also referred to as the 'Satanic S'. This was the symbol used by the Nazi SS.

666:
Number of the Great Beast or Anti-Christ, in its various forms (Rev. 13:18). It is a common form of tattoo used by occultists.

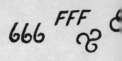

Ankkh
Egyptian symbol of life, often associated with fertility.

Inverted cross
Sometimes called 'Southern Cross' sym-bolises mockery and rejection of the cross of Christ. It is often seen in the form of earrings and necklaces, on album covers or in graffiti or tattoos.

Black mass indicator
Both symbols can be used to indicate a
Black Mass – a satanic practice parody-
ing the Catholic Mass. During a Black
Mass, holy items are defiled and illegal
activities performed including sacrifice
of unbaptised infants and the reciting
of the Lord's Prayer backwards.

Cross of confusion
First used by Romans who questioned
the truth of Christianity.

Church of Satan
Can be found in Anton La Vey's Satanic
Bible above the 'Nine Satanic Statements'. Many adolescents are using this
in notebooks, graffiti and in self-made
tattoos.

Emblem of baphomet
Strictly used by satanists and considered
a demonic deity symbolic of the devil.
Note the inverted pentagram forms the
goat-head.

Sometimes teenagers will write words, sentences and even
whole letters backwards. For example:

NATAS/SATAN	NEMA/AMEN	REDRUM/MURDER
EVIL/LIVE	MAD DOG/GOD DAM	SUSEJ/JESUS

Sometimes territory i.e. a house, a church, or specific area
which is to be the focus of occult activity/ritual/target for
cursing is marked out. Such markings can be of coloured
paper/ribbon/foil hung on hedges, gates, fences or walls.

Trail markers indicating locations or directions are used
by occultists. These may be unique to one particular coven,
or in more general use. There may be just a pentagram

scrawled on a wall, roadside or building to indicate a site where occult activity may take place, e.g.:

  THE CIRCLE = starting point

  RISING/FALLING LINE = direction and type of terrain.

Chapter 8

Pathway to Victory

It is not enough that God should make a promise to His people; they must claim its fulfilment and put themselves at His disposal, that it may be fulfilled through them. The ancient prediction that the kingdoms of this world shall become the kingdom of our Lord is true, but we must pray for and hasten its advent.

(F. B. Meyer)[4]

The final battle for David came when, as an old man unable to rule and scarcely able to walk, he was told of the attempt by another of his sons to usurp the throne. But David's throne had been promised to Solomon by God, and it was only the quick action of Nathan and Bathsheba that saved the day. The moment they heard that Adonijah had proclaimed himself king, they immediately went to David to remind him of his promise to Solomon. It is on that subject that Meyer makes his comment.

The importance of prayer

Sometimes we wonder how to pray or if our prayers really make a difference. After all, can we change the mind of God? Sometimes it might seem like it, but more accurately, I feel, it would be truer to say that God waits for us to cooperate with Him and to claim the promises that He has given. There are times in the Scriptures where God has expressed sorrow, and astonishment that there was no one to intercede: 'And he saw that there was no man, and wondered that there was no intercessor' (Isa. 59:16 AV). In Ezekiel 22:30 we read: 'I looked for a man among them who would build up the wall and stand before me in the gap on behalf of the land so that I would not have to destroy it, but I found none.' In the New Testament we are told, 'You do not have, because you do not ask God' (James 4:2). On the more positive side, God has specifically told us to ask Him for certain things. 'Call to me and I will answer you and tell you great and unsearchable things you do not know' (Jer. 33:3). We are shown in the book of Daniel that when Daniel saw that the seventy years of captivity had been completed, and yet the promised deliverance had not come, he set himself to fast and pray. The result? God used Cyrus as His chosen instrument to let the people return to their homeland. What happened? Had God forgotten? No, never. But as part of our growth in faith, He will wait for us to claim His promises and call into being the things that are yet unseen. What a tremendous privilege that God should call us to be workers together with Him!

Today it does seem as though God is raising up some strategic prayer initiatives throughout the world, and there is increasing emphasis on spiritual warfare. Recently I had the privilege of being in Seoul, the capital of South Korea, attending a Global Conference on world evangelisation. While I was there I had the opportunity, with a number of other delegates, to attend the world's largest church, with over 700,000 members, who are making an impact on their community. And one could say they have had an impact on their nation as, after much specific prayer by the church, they now have a largely Christian government. How did this all come about? The church started in an old army surplus tent with Pastor Dr Yonggi Cho's family and a few neighbours. From there they prayed themselves into what they are now. The result of prayer and spiritual warfare in that place is that hundreds are coming to Christ all the time. I attended the second service of the day, at 9 a.m., which was billed as a 'guest service'. After a wonderful teaching sermon, literally hundreds all over the church stood up to give their lives to Christ. Do we have faith enough to believe this could happen here in England?

David's passion for God

David was called 'a man after God's own heart' (Acts 13:22), and I believe that since he was such a man, he knew much of the heart of God. We have seen how he sought His guidance, how he sang His praises, how he encouraged himself in God when the situation was desperate. And we can be tempted to look at David and think it was all right for him. But was it? As I have been writing this book, I have marvelled at and have been challenged by the thought that God uses such flawed characters and makes them great as they submit to His will and His discipline.

David had many things against him. He came from a very difficult home, probably not out of the same 'drawer' as his brothers, misunderstood and roughly treated by them, and not especially favoured by his elderly father, to whom he may have been an embarrassment. He was the object of intense and violent jealousy, and his life was threatened many times. He was despised by his wife, Michal, and for a man with a nature like David's that could have been totally destructive.

He became a brilliant soldier and leader, able to take a bunch of social misfits and turn them into a highly disciplined army of professional soldiers, successful in all they did. And yet he was unable to control and discipline his own sons. His own moral failures would doubtless have haunted him all his life – his adultery with Bathsheba and his murder of Uriah, and the violent and needless slaughter from his hideout in Ziklag when he was on the run from Saul. One can understand why he wrote Psalms 32 and 51, his great prayers of contrition.

I have often wondered if the key to David's life with God is not to be found in Psalm 27:4: 'One thing I ask of the LORD, this is what I seek: that I may dwell in the house of the LORD all the days of my life, to gaze upon the beauty of the LORD and to seek him in his temple.' David was a man who had a single vision and passion, and that was for God. Yes, he strayed and did all the things listed above and received God's chastening. But underneath it all I believe there was that passion for God which will lead to a closer walk with Him and to knowing something of the secrets of His heart. May that be the longing of us all.

Obey the promptings to pray

David was also a man who listened to God and wrote, 'My heart says of you, "Seek his face!" Your face, LORD, I will seek' (Ps. 27:8). We have seen the importance of hearing from God, but sometimes in our frantic modern life we often don't take the time, or if we hear God prompting us, we either ignore it or put it off for later, when it may be too late.

When I was teaching at the Bible College, Saturday was a day off for staff and students. On one particular Saturday, a glorious summer day, I was at the home of my brother and sister-in-law sunbathing in their garden. Suddenly I had a tremendous urge to pray for one particular student. I hadn't been thinking about her and there was no special reason that I knew of for me to urgently pray for her, but the burden was there. I prayed around several things that might have been the problem, but none of them seemed right until I found myself praying for her physical safety. I knew in my spirit that that was right. I prayed on for about thirty minutes until the burden lifted. The next day, back at College, I told the student of my burden for her and asked if anything special had happened to her. She immediately thanked me for praying and said that although she could not go into details, what I had prayed was right on target.

Let us obey those promptings at once. Maybe we are feeling especially troubled suddenly and churned up inside. Pray at once about it and for God's protection and deliverance. Don't let it go on unchecked. I have learned to take seriously these 'feelings', as they have often been

the forerunner of some bad situation that could have been
saved by prayer. We do not know what is ahead of us, but
the Holy Spirit does, and often He will prompt us to pray
about something we are unaware of and we will receive the
protection of angels.

One time before speaking at a meeting, while a group of
us were praying beforehand, I had a strong sense of the
approach of something evil. I had no idea what it was, but
cried out to the Lord in my spirit, and after a while the
sensation went and the meeting was blessed. But without my
crying to God we could have been under demonic attack.

The power of praise

When we are thinking in terms of spiritual warfare, what
more wonderful assurance can we have than that which
David had: 'in the day of trouble he will keep me safe in
his dwelling; he will hide me in the shelter of his tabernacle
and set me high upon a rock. Then my head will be exalted
above the enemies who surround me; at his tabernacle will
I sacrifice with shouts of joy; I will sing and make music
to the LORD' (Ps. 27:5–6).

One of the most important weapons we have in spiritual
warfare is the weapon of praise. Satan hates to hear us
praise God, and as we do we weaken the demonic powers
and shake the principalities. The walls of Jericho fell at the
shout of praise, and many of the walls that surround us and
seek to imprison us can be flattened by the shout of praise. A
general who was writing about his principles of warfare once
stated that it was more important to destroy the courage of
the enemy's troops than to destroy his troops. In spiritual
warfare praise, worship and proclaiming Scripture not only
give us confidence, but they also devastate the morale and
will to resist of the evil spirits.

When Jesus was on earth His very presence struck terror
into demons, and they had to obey His command. When
the demon-possessed man of Gadara met Jesus, we read
that he immediately fell at His feet and cried out, '"What
do you want with me, Jesus, Son of the Most High God? I

beg you, don't torture me!" For Jesus had commanded the
evil spirit to come out of the man' (Luke 8:28–29). As we
call upon the Name of Jesus and uplift Him in praise, we
prepare the way for God's intervention. In Psalm 50:23 we
read, 'He who sacrifices thank-offerings honours me, and
he prepares the way so that I may show him the salvation
of God.' In the Authorised Version the first phrase reads,
'Whoso offereth praise glorifieth me . . .' At a later time in
the history of Judah we read that King Jehoshaphat, when
faced with a formidable array of enemies, following Divine
direction, put singers in front of the army to praise God as
they went out to battle, resulting in a great victory:

> After consulting the people, Jehoshaphat appointed
> men to sing to the LORD and to praise him for the
> splendour of his holiness as they went out at the head of
> the army, saying: 'Give thanks to the LORD, for his love
> endures for ever.' As they began to sing and praise, the
> LORD set ambushes against the men of Ammon and
> Moab and Mount Seir who were invading Judah, and
> they were defeated.
>
> (2 Chron. 20:21–22)

At a time when David could have been utterly defeated and
even killed – his men spoke of stoning him after they returned
to Ziklag and found the place burned down and their wives
and children gone – we read that instead David encouraged
himself in the Lord. Maybe he sang one of his psalms and
played his harp. We don't know, but we are told he was
encouraged and helped by praising the Lord. Please note
that it does not say that he spent valuable time berating
himself and saying it was his fault. It most certainly was
his fault, and he knew it and the men knew it, but that
was not the focus of his attention. God was his focus, and
so his private battle was won. Because of that he was able
to enquire of the Lord, and get directions as to what to
do, which he followed carefully, resulting in everything and
everyone being recovered. A successful end to what seemed
a disastrous situation.

How often Satan can ensnare us by making us feel guilty, and we stay trapped in that state, instead of coming to the One who can cleanse, forgive and move us on to victory. How do we do that? Certainly, where confession and repentance are needed, let us do that without delay, and then let us thank God and praise Him even for allowing a difficult situation so that we can prove Him in a way we never could have done without it. That sort of thinking really makes the devil mad! And, more importantly, it will also allow God to work in and through us in ways that will bring glory to Him and growth to us.

Praise helps us to be strong in the Lord, like David's mighty men. In 2 Samuel 23 we read about Eleazar, who alone stood against the Philistines when Israel retreated: 'but he stood his ground and struck down the Philistines till his hand grew tired and froze to the sword. The LORD brought about a great victory that day' (verse 10). Then there was Shammah: 'When the Philistines banded together . . . Israel's troops fled from them. But Shammah took his stand in the middle of the field. He defended it and struck the Philistines down, and the LORD brought about a great victory.'

'Abishai . . . raised his spear against three hundred men' (verse 18). Benaiah struck down two of Moab's best men; and he killed a lion in a pit on a snowy day and struck down a huge Egyptian: 'Although the Egyptian had a spear in his hand, Benaiah went against him with a club. He snatched the spear from the Egyptian's hand and killed him with his own spear' (verse 21).

What do we learn from these four men who were special bodyguards of David? Like the young David when he faced Goliath, they probably had that sense of exactly who the enemy was that they were fighting – an enemy defying the Lord God. It's interesting to note that once again in the face of the Philistines Israel fled. Sometimes we feel like fleeing in the face of satanic attack, when Satan faces us like a roaring lion, and yet if our hearts are right with God, we know we are protected by the blood of Christ, the Word of God, the Spirit of God and the armour of God, and so we should be like these men and stand our ground. As Paul admonished us, 'and after you have done everything, to stand' (Eph. 6:13).

I like the description of Benaiah, who 'went down into a pit on a snowy day and killed a lion' (2 Sam. 23:20). What a precarious situation. Facing a lion is bad enough – but in that weather! God is able to make even our feet to be firm and not slip when we trust Him. These men were strong and brave because they knew who they were serving. David was a fearless warrior, and they would have seen him in action many times. The same is true for us. When we know who we are in Christ, and all that Christ has done for us, and the power available to us, then we need never be afraid of Satan – he is afraid of us!

We have all the authority of the Word of God, the power that raised Christ from the dead dwelling in us – the Holy Spirit – and the all-powerful Name of Jesus, against which the demons cannot stand.

David's commitment . . . and ours?

In Chapter 2 we saw how David sinned by numbering his army, either through pride or fear and lack of reliance on God. This resulted in three days of terrible plague which took the lives of 70,000 people. David deeply repented of this as he agonisingly watched the ravages being made on his nation because of his sin. As Jerusalem was about to be destroyed because of it, God stopped the destroying angel at the threshing floor of Araunah on Mount Moriah, the very place where 850 years before Abraham had offered his son Isaac, and where later Solomon was to build the most magnificent Temple that has ever been seen.

Only when David saw the avenging angel with his drawn sword over Jerusalem did he realise the full extent of his sin, and he cried to God for mercy: 'When David saw the angel who was striking down the people, he said to the LORD, "I am the one who has sinned and done wrong. These are but sheep. What have they done? Let your hand fall upon me and my family"' (2 Sam. 24:17). But the results of this sin had taken their toll. Philip Keller, commenting on this story, says:

> If more men and women truly saw the gravity of their sins against God, they would desist from evil. But they do not. A large portion of the responsibility for sin being so rampant in our society is that our leaders will not cry out against it. Rather, they merely protest with pious platitudes that people are 'sick', that they 'hurt', and what they need is soft sympathy, rather than heart changing repentance.[5]

As the avenging angel stopped at the threshing floor of Araunah, the prophet Gad told David to build an altar there. Araunah felt honoured by this, and on hearing that David wanted to buy his threshing floor to offer sacrifices, he immediately told David that he could have everything – the threshing floor, the oxen and the wood for the sacrifice – for nothing. A truly magnanimous gesture on Araunah's part. What a temptation. But not to David. David knew his God, and all that He had done for him over the many eventful years of his life; David remembered His love and protection, His dealings with him in the valley of the shadow of death, and in providing him with a banquet in the face of his enemies – a God who was rich in mercy and worthy of all honour. Not a God of the second best, because He had never given David His second best – there's no such thing with God. So David gave his classic reply: 'I will not sacrifice to the LORD my God burnt offerings that cost me nothing' (2 Sam. 24:24). And he paid Araunah very handsomely.

David was a man who longed after God, as we saw in Psalm 27:4. He also said, 'O God, you are my God, earnestly I seek you; My soul thirsts for you, my body longs for you' (Ps 63:1). He knew where to turn when the going was tough: 'Hear my cry, O God; listen to my prayer. From the ends of the earth I call to you, I call as my heart grows faint; lead me to the rock that is higher than I' (Ps. 61:1–2). He was a man who knew the heights of joy and success as well as the depths of sorrow and rejection. Though he was a man after God's own heart, he also knew the bitterness of sin in his life and the consequences of it; he knew what it was to wrestle with guilt and then to know the joy of forgiveness. All of this was costly for him as it is for us, because we are in a battle, and battles are costly.

But the greatest cost in this battle has already been paid by God, who sent His own Son to die on the cross, and by Jesus, who on the cross bore all our sins and was forsaken by His Father at that moment when all the sins of the world were laid upon Him. David saw this prophetically in Psalm 22, the Psalm that graphically depicts the crucifixion: 'My God, my God, why have you forsaken me?' (verse 1).

Though victory is assured, the battle is still on, and we are to 'fight the good fight' and strongly resist the evil one. If we are serious about seeing victory in our own lives and about people being brought into the kingdom, then let us be serious about our own commitment to the Lord. There is a cost involved – and yet how small it is compared to the cost of Calvary and to the reward awaiting us. Let us pay the price of commitment and enjoy the victory. Thus we will fulfil our destiny – we were created to conquer.

Appendix I

Prayers for Use in Spiritual Warfare

A prayer of victory and praise

Here are some of David's words of victory and praise from
2 Samuel 22 which we can proclaim when we are under
attack from our spiritual enemy:

> The LORD is my rock, my fortress and my deliverer;
> my God is my rock, in whom I take refuge,
> my shield and the horn of my salvation.
> He is my stronghold, my refuge and my saviour –
> from violent men you save me.
> I call to the LORD, who is worthy of praise,
> and I am saved from my enemies . . .
>
> He reached down from on high and took hold of me;
> he drew me out of deep waters.
> He rescued me from my powerful enemy,
> from my foes, who were too strong for me.
> They confronted me in the day of my disaster,
> but the LORD was my support.
> He brought me out into a spacious place;
> he rescued me because he delighted in me . . .
>
> As for God, his way is perfect;
> the word of the LORD is flawless.
> He is a shield
> for all who take refuge in him.

For who is God besides the LORD?
And who is the Rock except our God?
It is God who arms me with strength
and makes my way perfect . . .

The LORD lives! Praise be to my Rock!
Exalted be God, the Rock, my Saviour!
He is the God who avenges me,
who puts the nations under me,
who sets me free from my enemies . . . I will sing
  praises to your name . . .

A prayer for personal deliverance

Lord Jesus Christ, I believe that you are the Son of God
and the only way to God; that you died on the cross for my
sins and that you rose again from the dead that I might be
forgiven and receive eternal life. And now, Lord Jesus, you
know my problem, you know the darkness in my life, the
frustration, things that I cannot even name, but you know
them. I thank you, Lord Jesus, that you were made a curse
that I might be delivered and receive the blessing.

I turn from all known sin. I turn from everything satanic.
I turn from all occult involvement. I forgive every other
person who ever harmed me or wronged me. I forgive them
all as I would have God forgive me.

Now, Lord Jesus, in simple faith I receive your forgiveness. I receive the cleansing of your blood and in your
Almighty Name, I loose myself now from any curse that
is over my life or my family. I loose myself in the Name
of Jesus. Amen.

A prayer for the cleansing and dedicating of homes

Read aloud Psalm 91, and then these extracts from
Deuteronomy:

> There is no-one like the God of Jeshurun,
> who rides on the heavens to help you
> and on the clouds in his majesty.

The eternal God is your refuge,
and underneath are the everlasting arms.
He will drive out your enemy before you,
saying, 'Destroy him!'
So Israel will live in safety alone;
Jacob's spring is secure
in a land of grain and new wine,
where the heavens drop dew.
Blessed are you, O Israel!
Who is like you,
a people saved by the LORD?
He is your shield and helper
and your glorious sword.
Your enemies will cower before you,
and you will trample down their high places.

(Deut. 33:26–29)

The Lord has promised that as we obey Him, 'You will be blessed when you come in and blessed when you go out. The LORD will grant that the enemies who rise up against you will be defeated before you. They will come at you from one direction but flee from you in seven' (Deut. 28:6–7).

Then read aloud Romans 8:31–39.

A binding prayer for spiritual protection

In the Name of Jesus Christ, by the power of His cross and blood, we bind the spirits, powers and forces of the earth, the underground, the air, the water, the fire, the nether world and the satanic forces of nature.

We rebuke any curses, and bless those who curse us.

We bind all demonic interplay, interaction and communication.

We claim the protection of the shed blood of Jesus Christ over . . . (the person).

We call on the power, the presence of the Holy Spirit to fill this room, to fill (the person) and to guide our prayers.

We also call on the presence of the holy angels, the ministry of angels. Amen. (This can be prayed in the first person and for yourself.)

(When a friend of mine felt that her home was particularly under attack, with the continual illnesses of her children and a burglary, she prayed through her home, putting a touch of red wine on the doors and windows (grape juice could also be used), symbolising the blood of Christ for protection, and she claimed the promise of Exodus 12:22–23 that the destroyer would pass over. She said she noticed a considerable difference in the atmosphere in the home after that, and her children's health improved considerably.)

Appendix II

Further Reading

Neil T. Anderson, *Victory over the Darkness Realizing the Power of your Identity in Christ*

Neil T. Anderson, *The Bondage Breaker*

Evelyn Christenson, *Battling the Prince of Darkness*

Francis Frangipane, *The Three Battlegrounds*

Cindy Jacobs, *Possessing the Gates of the Enemy*

Gary D. Kinnaman, *Overcoming the Dominion of Darkness*

Campbell McAlpine, *The Practice of Biblical Meditation*

Frank E. Peretti, *This Present Darkness*

Derek Prince, *Blessing or Curse: You Can Choose*

Charles Spurgeon, *Spiritual Warfare in a Believer's Life*

C. Peter Wagner, *Warfare Prayer: Strategies for Combating the Rulers of Darkness*

C. Peter Wagner, *Prayer Shield: Praying for Christian Leaders*

Tom White, *The Believer's Guide to Spiritual Warfare*

Notes

1 F. B. Meyer, *Devotional Bible Commentary* (Tyndale House Pub. Inc., 1989), p. 138.
2 David Stoop and James Masteller, *Forgiving Our Parents and Forgiving Ourselves: Healing Adult Children of Dysfunctional families* (Servant Publications, Ann Arbor, Michigan, 1991), p. 32.
3 Neil Anderson, *Victory Over Darkness* (Monarch Publications, Crowborough, 1992), pp. 12–13.
4 Meyer, *Devotional Bible Commentory*, p. 151.
5 Philip Keller, *David the Shepherd King*, vol. II (Word Books, Milton Keynes, 1992), p. 195.